THE ACCIDENTAL ANTHOLOGY

A WORK-THROUGH-IT COLLECTION FOR ADULTS
BY
TK LONG

THE ACCIDENTAL ANTHOLOGY Copyright © 2020 by TK Long.

ARTIST ACKNOWLEDGEMENTS

COVER AND COLORING PAGES

ALEXANDRIA BISHOP

PHOTOGRAPHY
DAN HOGMAN
MICHELLENE FRYSON
REGGIE RAPHAEL WALLACE
SAMANTHA MAYER
FREDDE DAVIS-EVANS

TABLE OF CONTENTS

Voice of the Brokenhearted 1
Let Me Be Your Refuge 4
For Page & Poem 5
Cool 6
Sick 7
I Got A Blues In My Soul 8
The Truth About Women 10
Dat Black Man 11
I Always Identify With Broken Things 12
You've Got Me 13
Unrequited (Been There?) 14
Unpretty II 16
It Happens In The Bathroom 18
I Am Trayvon Martin 22
Monika 25
When Lauryn Was Late 26
Beauty 27
Music Man 28
Legs 30
Naked 31
My Body 32
Why Couldn't You Be Pretty? 34
Sing 35
The Nurse 36
Homeboy 38
'Til Death: A One-Woman Deception 39
Homeboy Revisited 41
Miss Mabel Watches Television 44
Land Of The... 46
Nigger 47
Fruitless 49
Family Tree 50
The Haunting of George Zimmerman 53
I Wanted To Write You A Thank You Note 55
Careful, Or You'll Be In My Next Novel 56
The Whore of Corporate America 57
The Wrong Alice 59
Hurts Like New Shoes 60
Trust Fall 62
Why I Hated Gabrielle Union And What She Taught Me About Myself 63
The Wait 66
Taking Back My Freedom 68
Exit Stage Left 71
Sinners Got Souls Too (An Alice Walker Inspiration) 76
Miss Used And Abused 93
Morning Routine 94
The Doors 96
The Shoulders I Stand On 98
Who Needs A Song? 99
& 100

My G-Bird 102
My Mama 103
Dear White Best Friend 104
Braelynn 105
Lying On Your Face 106
I Had A Visitor 108
A Groove For Midnight 110
A Lesson In Lilies 112
In His Hair 113
Acceptance 114
Bubba 116
Moments For Life 118
Goodbye Forever 119
Thirsty 120
Drunk 122
Live To Dream (In Memory of the Beautiful Souls Of Pulse Orlando) 123
Sometimes 126
Everything and Nothing 127
Lock & Key 128
Happy Valentine's Day 129
Bobby 131
Sometimes I Am Love 133
If Only 134
What Is Music? 135
Slippery Slope 136
Just Another Shade of Pretty 137
Take Me or Leave Me 138
Awake 139
Love Me Right 141
ATM 142
Dismembered 143
Dahlia 144
4am 146
Mama Said 148
Holly 149
Strange Fruit 150
Once Upon A Time 152
You're Here 154
Through The Looking Glass 155
Lady on the Bench 156
I'm In Love 157
In Passing 159
The Vein 161
You 163
Someone You Used To Know 164
Your Truth 165
The Prenup 166

Baggage Claim 167
So Sorry 168
Theory on Saturn 169
U.B. (Unapologetically Black) 170
Ticket to Ride 172
Don't Stop Dancing 173
Marry Me Tomorrow 174
Intergalactic 175
Forbidden Words 176
Perfect Stranger 177
Glass Houses 178
Michelle 179
November 8, 2016 181
I Don't Want to Write 182
Bare 183
Nina in Variation 184
Purple Heart 186
Real Love 187
Black Child 188
I Hate U 189
Love Song 190
Burned 193
Let Love Rule 194
The Shit 195
Her (At The Airport) 198
Pieces 199
Graveyard 201
Hunger Pains 202
Tools of War 203
Pep Talk 204
Hey, Kalief 206
About The Sky 208
Freedom 209
Safety 210
5 A.M. 211
I Made You A Mixtape 212
For REAL 215
Priceless 216
Paul Revere 217
What Happened to Sandra Bland? 218
Grand Canyon 219
On Writing 221
Shamika 222
Princess Nobody 223
Good Riddance 224
Build 226
Secret of the Sun 227
Staring At Staff Paper 228
Lost One 229
Changed 230
Signs 231

Transplant 232
Running in Place 233
WHOAman 234
Invested 235
Black Man 236
Not Anymore 237
Broken Lines 238
Nothing Compares 2 U 239
No Love 240
Come Closer 241
Unpacking 242
Love 243
Happily Never After 244
Be Art 245
After Church 246
Not the Girl 249
The Sorry You Didn't Say 250
'Round Midnight 251
Ashes To Ashes: The Case for Cremation 252
Sentimental Mood 254
Zora 255
Forget Me Lots 256
Be Free 257
The Beautiful Struggle 258
Functional 259
Up 260
Black People 261
The Other Woman 263
Ms. Cellophane 264
Don't Give Up 265
Liquidity 266
Little One 267
Still The Wrong Alice 268
Mirror 269
Apparition 271
He Was Music 272
REVOLution 274
How To Love 275
Nope 276
Dazed & Confused (Thinking In My Garage) 277
Anachronistic 278
Home 279
Black 280
Slow Dance 281
Lear 282

VOICE OF THE BROKENHEARTED

I am the voice of the brokenhearted.
I speak for the little girl whose father
Didn't love her enough
And for the classmate whose father
Loved her too well, too often and too passionately.
I speak for the boy who could have been in the NFL
If his parents could have afforded the cleats.

I speak for the ones who wanted to
Heal the world, but have been called
Too stupid, too poor or too Black.

I speak for that teacher who could
Create world leaders if the parents would
Stop treating the classroom like enemy lines
(Their accusations and "My child would never" speeches are the best disguised WMDs ever.
I speak for the girl who thinks of
Her third-grade teacher calling her "Chunk"
As she binges and purges.
I speak for the guy called crazy as he burns
Love letters from the love of his life
Who slept with his best friend.
I speak for him as he throws away the
Ring and goes to spend some quality time
With his tears and his rifle.
I speak for those children who always heard
They were not good enough and had no one
To convince them otherwise.
I speak for the girl who opened her heart and got rejected,
So, she opened her legs repeatedly
And the world closed all windows of opportunity.
I speak for those who are not free to love their lovers
Because society can't see past genitalia and see hearts and souls.
I speak for the faithful mother of three
Whose husband wouldn't give her another baby
But brought her full-blown AIDS with a shiny red bow.
I speak for that man whose child support
Turns into Mama's new Gucci,
But on Father's Day, makes him a
"No good, ain't shit deadbeat".
I speak for the man who has been told he
Needs to make six figures to win the
Affection of a woman who will
Leave him as soon as a zero falls off.
I speak for that husband at home with

The kids while his wife is out
Raising her skirt and lowering her standards.
I speak for that woman who had company
In her bed, but never realized she was all alone in love.
I am the voice of the beaten,
The downtrodden and the damned.
I am the poet.
I am the hand that writes the world.

TK

Why do you do what you do? What/Who is your "why"?

LET ME BE YOUR REFUGE

Let me be your refuge.
Let me be the place where you take off your skin
And let your insides glow.
Know that you can hide yourself in me
And I will find beauty in your secrecy.
Know that you can tell me your deepest thoughts
And I will help polish your mind.
Let me be the place where dark becomes light
And senselessness rests comfortably on the lines of rationality.
Let me be the place where old cuts of love and disappointment
Become new grooves of peace and sensuality.
Let me be the place where you collapse in fits
Of orgasmic satisfaction.
Let me be your someday.
Let me be your forever.
Let me be your joy.
Let me be yours.

TK

FOR PAGE & POEM

Come here.
Let me talk to you.
Let me scrawl my sweet nothings
Upon you.
Let me press you to my lips and
Infuse you with desire.
Let me have my way as well as those
Unfathomable with you.
All of you.
I will leave no space untouched.
Let me press myself to you
And share with you my heartbeat.
Let me run my fingers down your body
So that you quake with anticipation.
Then I will open myself to you
And let you do what you will.
Navigate me.
Press deep
And mold yourself to me.
Scope out every nook and cranny
And find a spot you like.
Rest there and make something happen.
Explode in me and make me sing your praises.
Stay with me forever.

TK

COOL

sit back, sweet thang
and let me lay some of this ol' cool on you
don't try and block me wit' none of that
i already got a man jive
cause what yo man is brangin
can't top none of what I got
say mama, step ova heyah in dis co'nah
wit me
let me entice ya wit my words
bet you ain't neva heard no tongue slick as mine befo'
see sweet mama, they call me cool
but it ain't the same cool you get from dem fans at
yo mama's house
i'm the kinda cool dat might breathe fuh two seconds
and charm ya right out ya clothes
i'm da kinda cool dat will have you givin up all yo paychecks just cause
I'm givin' up dis good lovin'
I'm da kinda cool you'll wish would neva leave
but sho' nuff beg to stay
my suits stay clean
my hats stay tipped
and mama you'll never stray when you kiss dese lips
I'm cool
I got bright eyes and a smile
dat neva go wrong
and baby my cadillac
ain't da only thang dat's long
I told ya'
I'm cool
i'll put lovin' thoughts all up in yo' head
girl they write stories bout how
i've been known to rock a bed

just *coooooooooool*.......

when my hands rest upon yo chest you'll
be convinced
of all the power I possess
too damn cool
we can phone, bone
and i'll take you home
but when you talk about marriage i'll
have to leave you alone
i told you I'm cool
now really, can you dig it?

TK

SICK

You…make…me…sick.
I admit it.
You're like a disease.
You're an infectious growth on my heart.
My mind coughs and instantly you know everything that
Is in my soul.
My body sneezes loudly and brings forth a heavy
Downpour of emotion.
I am feverish with the notion of loving you.
I ache miserably when you're not around.
Cold sweats anoint me during the times I miss you most.
I lie in my bed of sorrow but pull the covers of defense tight
Under my chin.
I…am…sick.
My pride acts as an antibody, fighting off every
Thought of you.
It stands strongly against all your gloriously
Persistent germs.
I must fight this.
Visions of kissing you are my chicken soup, the antidote for my affliction.
Thoughts of being in your arms are warm cups of tea, filler
For my every void.
But seeing your face and kissing your lips are the only things
That can cure me.
The congestion of my heart will only clear up when I meet your embrace.
Your voice will be a new drug and
Bring me euphoria.
I'm sick with you.
You're like a disease-
The precious ailment I want forever.

TK

I GOT A BLUES IN MY SOUL

I got a blues in my soul
That none of you can hear.
I sing it in triumph.
I sing it in fear.
I sing it in a hurry.
I sometimes sing it slow.
I sing it in a language
You will never know.

My song breaks my heart.
It puts me back together.
My song is one that may
Go on and on forever.
My song builds me up.
It breaks me down too.
My song is about all the things that
I can and cannot do.
It is my happy medium.
It is my level plain.
It is everything I have lost and all
I stand to gain.

Please hear me out.
The blues isn't always a bad thing.
You'd understand this perfectly
If you could only hear me sing.
.

TK

"One good thing about music, when it hits, you feel no pain." -Bob Marley

THE TRUTH ABOUT WOMEN

Many of us are beautiful houses filled with broken furniture. On the outside, we are these majestic structures that stand tall and add character to the streets we stand on. But when you open our doors, you walk in to chairs that are broken for fear that someone may want to stay a while, cracked mirrors for fear of our own pasts and dusty tables because our cupboards are void of the food we should have to nourish ourselves when our souls are hungry. We have been lived in and not taken care of and a new tenant who may very well be worthy is often left to clean up behind the last and bear the burden of their negligence. Our beds have been slept in and there are often times that we thought the ones who have occupied them were doing us a favor by taking on the chore of making them. But we were too blind to see that they made them with dirty sheets and we've inherited bedbugs that will never leave. When we are sad, we turn on our faucets and flood every room we have over someone who isn't really worth a glass of our tears. We fire up our ovens and make meals for those who deserve to choke on their own lies. There are several levels to our staircases and sometimes depending on how pretty the picture looks as someone is climbing them, we may ignore the creaks and loud warning signs that occur beneath their feet. They trek through our family rooms and pay no mind to the pictures on the mantle or how we have strategically left a place for them and their children when we could have easily filled those spaces with more love for ourselves or someone who actually WANTED to be there. We keep the thickest layers of dust on our windows because we are too embarrassed about the condition of our quarters and are leery of those trying to peek through them and place something shiny but of little to no value in our foyers thinking they can "spruce up the place". There have been many so-called "maintenance men" who have come through. But their stucco, putty, rugs and wallpaper only cover the cracks, holes, dents and scratches that happen as a result of quarrels with the ones responsible for our deplorable condition. Our yards are large with lots of potential, but the fact that they have seen no water causes their bruised brown grasses to crawl in every direction to quench their lingering thirsts. When someone leaves, we lock our gates and hope to never have another visitor. When another mansion stands next to us, we slap some paint on our shutters and try to pull ourselves together so that it does not show how diminished our property value has become. Meanwhile, the wails of our hearts echo down the corridors singing a sad and all too familiar song.

TK

DAT BLACK MAN

"You know I seen a black man in a suit befo'. Looked real important, he did. The way he stepped high and talked to white folks just like he had business doin' it. His skin was shiny and smooth and he had a bright smile what look like he knowed somethin' I didn't. But I ain't neva seent a man lak dis one befo'. He stand strong and proud and make everybody feel lak dey got somethin' to live fo'. I wonder how he do dat. He sit and thank and come up wit' plans dat might change da whole worl' if somebody'll just let him."

TK

Photo by TK Long

I ALWAYS IDENTIFY WITH BROKEN THINGS

I always identify with broken things-
Having pieces of you lying in unknown...
Being forced to uselessness by way of separation,
Knowing the bigger part of you is somewhere else.
You serve no purpose because so much of you is missing.
You only bring frustration to others because of your own worthlessness.
You tend to get lost among the bigger things and become obsolete.
You're not whole, so none of you matters.
You're insignificant.
You're hopeless.
You're forgotten.

I always identify with broken things.

TK̀

YOU'VE GOT ME

You know you've got me gone, right?
Got me
Speeding the wrong way down one-way streets
In Matchbox cars
While shooting gumdrop guns
At paper airplanes that fly by.
Got me
Running down walls and up raindrops
Just before dancing naked
In the spotlights of spoons.
Got me
Painting pictures with erasers
And hanging them on liquid walls
In galleries no one has ever seen.
Got me
Braiding rainbows and putting them in my hair
And putting on invisible makeup
To get ready for the ball I wasn't invited to.
Got me
Staring at blank pages and seeing sounds
That I plan to put into a symphony
I will never compose.
Got me
Swimming in waterless pools
Next to bright white dragons
Got me
Taking nosedives off pyramids
And telling jokes to unicorns.
Oh yeah…
You've got me.

TK

UNREQUITED (BEEN THERE)?

Please apologize to your heart for me. It is not my intent to be cruel. I know that it seems that by simply being kind, I am letting you look at my heart while window shopping but refusing to put a price tag on it or ever allow you to take it home. But you see, after hours when the lights are turned out, I have spoken to my heart. I have told it you are kind and have good intentions, but I cannot convince it to love you romantically. I know the "just friends" garment does not fit you to your liking, but I simply see no reason to procure fabrics to weave you any other. It is my undying hope that the skirts I place around the issue of us being together will soften the blows of the truth. But deep down, I know that it won't. Often I have asked myself if I am horrid for not being able to find it in my heart to devote myself to someone who is kind and has good intentions. And again, I stand opposed of a heart I cannot convince to love you. I sometimes feel that by continuing to accept your friendship while longing for my true love, I am borrowing one soldier's inkwell to pen a love letter to his enemy. But this is the plight I must contend with. There is no doubt in my mind that I would feel the deepest regret for any time spent trying to convince myself to love you rather than doing what comes most natural with the one I am truly meant to love. And I do deem your friendship more valuable than a mere parting gift. So, rather than attempt to fall into a farce of love and have it end with you greeting me as a stranger with magnetism toward the blade of your sword, I must extend to you the truth and hope we can meet as two old friends crossing paths in the park. As a friend to you, my heart is an open fortress. As a lover, I can grant you no entry.

TK

Have you ever told someone you loved them but the feeling wasn't mutual? Or have you ever had to tell someone you didn't see them the way they saw you? How did that go?

_____
_____
_____
_____
_____
_____
_____
_____
_____
_____
_____
_____
_____

UNPRETTY II

Sometimes I cry because I don't like my eyes.
I feel they pale in comparison to hers.
Sometimes I cry because I dislike my thighs.
They're not as small as they once were.
At times, I hide because my lips are too big
And I feel they cheapen my smile.
Sometimes I'm upset that my butt is too big
And I can never achieve that certain style.
Sometimes I'm unhappy with the tone of my skin.
It's not as even as it should be.
I am disappointed blemish by blemish.
They are everywhere they possibly could be.
I'll never look like the girl in the magazine
Over whom men ogle and drool.
I'll never be that tall leggy model
Who turns scholars into her fools.
My belly's not flat,
My feet are too big
On bad mornings I look pretty rough.
My arms are too fat.
My nose is too round,
My eyelashes aren't quite long enough.
Teeth not a perfect white,
Heels not always high,
Not instantly admired,
Hair not always in place
No makeup on my face
I leave much to be desired.
"You have a beautiful soul"
"You've got a kind heart"
Is what you say to me
But when you measure
The true beauty of a woman
What do you really see?
It's the Paulas and Kims of the world
That you find synonymous with beauty.
Truthfully, you wouldn't give the time of day
To a girl who looks like me.
You scoff at my wide hips.
You laugh in my round face
When you see me, you see sex.

But when it comes to making life plans
You let go of my hand, skip, me and move right on to the next.
I'm not what you look for.
Instead it's those petite girls you seek.
Laxative junkies, slaves to the scale
And barely a cracker per week.
I'm not mad.
I'm not bashing you.
I'm just stating the facts.
Just let me speak my mind, say my piece
And say where I think your head's at.
Go on and get her.
She's your trophy.
Trim, toned and tall.
Don't feel guilty.
I'm alright.
And I'm not mad at all.
Just don't make things up.
Don't lie
Don't pretend you're attracted to me.
I'm a big girl
Who doesn't
Like being lied to
No matter how unpretty she might be.

TK

IT HAPPENS IN THE BATHROOM

Man in Blue: What time is it? Ugh, ten minutes until boarding. I am going to miss my flight. There's a line at the sinks. Who's gonna know If I don't wash? No one's looking. Maybe I can sneak out without drawing attention to myself. I have GOT to go. (door swings open)

Lady in Pink: No! No! No! No! No! No! No! No! Whew! JUST made it! Well, almost anyway. That is with the exception of that little puddle on the seat. As long as I don't get it on my dress, I'm good. That's all he cares about anyway. It is important that this date goes perfectly. Toilet flushed, hands washed, lipstick reapplied and PLEASE let's make sure he can't see these Spanx. I wonder if he missed me. (door swings open)

Man in Yellow: This…..damn….cough! I have had this cold for a week now and I can't seem to shake it. All day long just hack, hack, hack, a…..choo! Oh, shit. Just got something on the wall. Yeah. I could clean it off, but they don't pay me to do that. Let the cleaning crew earn their paychecks. Let me just grab a tissue and get out of here. (door swings open)

Photo by TK Long

Lady in Orange: Ssssh. Sssh. Ssssh. It's okay, Sweetie. I know a dirty diaper is not fun at all. I'll just lay you down here and change you before Daddy picks us up. See? You're smiling already. Who's Mommy's sweet boy? Who's Mommy's sweet b--(phone rings) Okay! Stop yelling! We're on the way out! (hangs up phone) I've got way too much to carry. I'll just leave that there. Someone will pick it up. (door swings open)

Lady in Black: John? Jared? Jim? What is his name? Who the hell cares when his lips are this soft? I wonder if that old lady next to us knows what we slipped away from the table to do? It doesn't really matter. She probably just wishes she remembers what it feels like. Damn, he's strong. Only used one hand to pick me up and push me against this wall. It's kinda cold against my ass. But that's the least of my worries. I just need to make sure the lady in the next stall doesn't hear me. What a night.

Man in Green: I will NEVER….drink…tequila again. I never knew what it felt like for your entire body to wage war against you. I feel like everything in me is trying TOOOOO-OOH-OOOOH (wretch… My God, when did I eat THAT?! Pull yourself together! Pull…yourself together. You are supposed to be here to celebrate your brother's promotion. Or was it your cousin breaking up with that crazy girlfriend of his? Or hell, maybe it's ChristMAAAAAHHHH (wretch). Speaking of Christmas, someone is going to get a nice surprise when they find this colorful package on the floor. I feel better now. Just had to get that outta me. Time to party. (door swings open)

Man in Red: Please, God! Please, Please, God! Please, God! Ugh! I really shoulda stopped at the sausage and peppers. Or I shoulda gotten up when the rumbling started. I think I got here just in the nick of time though. I'm really startin' to break a sweat here, but boy do I feel better. No toilet paper? What if I use one of them fancy towels they had by the door there? Nobody else in here but me. Guess I should shuffle out and get one. (shuffles to the door and back Yeah. That'll do it. (zips pants "All employees must wash hands before returning to work". Good thing I ain't an employee. Now let me at that dessert menu. (door swings open

TK

Speaking of washing your hands (or not), what is the biggest impact COVID-19 and the nationwide quarantine have had on you and your loved ones? What have you learned?

I AM TRAYVON MARTIN

Wet, murky, cold.
Grass against face
Helpless, stiff and paralyzed.
You know how you have those moments where
Everything feels like an out of body experience?
I think I might be having one now, but it feels a little more real this time.
I had a slight thirst before and had set out to quench it
That was a couple of hours ago.
I don't feel the thirst anymore though.
I don't really feel anything.
Everybody's crowded around me snapping pictures
Like I'm a celebrity.
But I can't remember anything I did to deserve it.
They are moving around using words like "gunshot",
"Wound", "Evidence" and "victim".
But there's no way they could be talking about me.
I'm pleading to them as loudly as I can
Somebody please come help me up.
It's cold out here and I'm all wet from the rain.
I guess I must have put on a few pounds since
This morning because I can't even lift myself.
This ground against my face is not the best feeling,
But I guess I'll wait until you finish before I ask for help again.
In the meantime, how am I gonna explain to my dad that
I didn't do the dishes because I played video games all day?
And I know my mom is gonna wonder why I'm so late
Calling her back. Maybe that was her texting me.
I heard my phone ring a few times, but I couldn't answer
For whatever reason.
I have a million things to do and a million calls I'd rather be
Making, but here I am, lying face down in the grass.
People are still taking pictures and
I hear one of them saying my name.
They're asking questions, but it's funny that no one bothers
To talk to me.
"He followed him around this corner and he saw him with his
Hands in the pocket of his hoodie."
Followed. Hands in the pocket of his hoodie.
Now that you mention it, I do remember that!
Yeah! I heard the dude behind me
But I didn't know what he wanted.

Maybe he thought I was up to something.
Young, Black. I guess I fit the profile.
I figured I better mention this creepy ass cracker to my
Friend, just in case he tried something.
I saw him looking at me a few minutes ago and he just
Didn't seem right.
All I had in my pocket was a bag of Skittles my step-brother
Asked for and the Watermelon Arizona I got for that
Thirst I told you about.
But he didn't know that.
I figured maybe if I put my hands in my pocket like I
Had a gun, he would put that together with young and Black
And leave me alone.
But, nah. This dude was up to something.
He gained on me and it looked like he had something in his hand.
Was that a gun?! Why pull a piece on a kid walking home
In the rain?
I heard my heart beating in my ears when he grabbed me.
My life flashed before my eyes and I knew I had to fight
For what was left of it.
Neighbors! They don't know me that well, but
Maybe if they hear me screaming, they'll come get
This dude off me.
Help! Heeeeeeeelp! Heeeeeeeeeeeeeeeelp!
I screamed so loud my lungs hurt.
Instead of somebody coming out, some weirdo sets
Off a firework.
Not like one of the Fourth of July combo ones,
But one.....single .. firework.
But I guess it was something about the firework
Because it made the dude stop what he was doing.
It must have been one loud ass firework too
Because I went deaf for a while after that.
As a matter of fact, before these people showed up,
That was the last thing I heard.
Now they are in a circle around me but I wonder if they
Even know that I can hear them.
They're asking about this one dude, a cop I think,
Who came over to me.
It looked like he was trying to give me mouth to mouth.
I never understood why he thought I needed it,
But he didn't really give me a chance to ask questions.
A whole lot of strange stuff had happened tonight.
These random people are asking about that scar on my knuckle.
It's a really funny story behind that.
I would be glad to tell it if they would just...help...me...UP!

Wait. What are they talking about?
"Bashed his head on the concrete"?
Who did that?! Did somebody show up to help me?!
"Slim jim"?!
Who needs a slim jim to go to the 7 Eleven?!
"Might have been high on something"?!
It's been DAYS since I smoked weed!
"Zimmerman feared for his life?!"
"Zimmerman"?! Is that the creepy cracker's name?! And HE was
The one with the gun! What did HE have to be scared of?!
Man, help me up, so I can tell y'all what REALLY happened!
Okay! Okay! Somebody must have heard me.
They're turning me over.
Okay. Here we go.
Wait. Something doesn't feel right.
What's going on with my chest?
The air just isn't circulating right.
It seems like it's passing straight through me.
It's not circulating at all.
And why am I so damn HEAVY?!
These people keep talking so loud!
I can't even think straight!
They keep going on and on about some "victim",
A "fatal gunshot wound", some "911 call" and the "time of dea--"
Wait. Everybody out here is looking at ME.
When they say "victim", they look at ME.
And for the "fatal gunshot wound", they keep
Pointing at that hole I never saw in my hoodie before.
Damn.
I should have called my mom
And done those dishes.
I should have explained those pictures of me on Facebook too.
I've never been a gangsta, but it was fun pretending.
Oh, and I probably should have pulled up my grades too.
I just hope that somebody tells my parents that I meant to.
That may not be as good as doing all that, but
There was no way I could have known that I would never get
The chance again.
I put this hoodie on to keep warm.
But nothing could have prepared me for this
Type of cold.

TK

MONIKA

Let me stand next to you
And draw from your strength.
Let me be strong enough to let
The pains of all the world wash over me.
Like a forgotten river of a far too
Distant past.
Let me be strong enough to ignore
The pressures upon my brain
And float through life
As light as a feather.
Let me be peaceful enough
To smile when it hurts to exist.
Let me be so humble that I do not
Amaze myself when I bear
Weight fit only for giants
Upon my human shoulders.
Let me be humble enough
To walk and not fly when
I have a heart fit for ten angels.
Let me take time from my day
To say kind words to a friend who
May be going through.
Let me be a blessing to the world.
A commodity.
A picture of true beauty.
If I was only able to let your strength
Flow through me
So that I may be at least half as strong.
To you I would be
Forever.
Grateful.

TK

WHEN LAURYN WAS LATE

At least the clocks worked right when Lauryn was late.
But look at us now.
Thursday is October and 3pm is Nevuary
And every moment feels like our Final Hour.
Remember when all we had to complain about was the
Show starting hours later when we had to work the next day?
Looking at the state of things now, we know we were the Lost Ones.
Right now we are hanging onto those jobs we would have
Played hookie from anyway by a thread.
Our babies are hungry and Every Ghetto, Every City
Feels the rumble in the bellies and the pains in their hearts
From the pandemic of racism that was already rampant
Before this one showed up.
We're depressed.
And When It Hurts So Bad that the pain becomes too big
For four walls, we take to the streets.
We know we risk health and safety but when you cry so
Loud your lungs bleed and still no one hears you,
Nothing Even Matters.
We have politicians telling us things are getting better
When we can see the lie.
Forgive Them Father. They know what they do.
But since it has always been in our nature,
We ask that you forgive them anyway.
When a mother loses her son to one of the two full grown
Beasts out there, then her tears become a sorrowful scroll
Of all the things she never got to Tell Him
And the daily news becomes a reminder of all the
Things she never will.
We're hurting and dying.
Now I kinda wish for the times when Lauryn was late.
At least things made a little more sense then.

TK

BEAUTY

I experience it like a lover's kiss.
Just the anticipation gives my cheeks a glow.
The closer it comes, the more I tingle and invite it.
Its warmth covers my mouth and travels within me.
Inside it rouses me and runs around knocking on the doors
I normally keep closed until I have company.
It flings open windows and lets in sunlight.
It sits down at the piano and calls the rest of me over.
It gives all of me that something to sing about that I have longed for.
It invites the neighbors over to watch me shine and hear my sweet soprano.
It sweeps me into its arms and spins me around my spirit.
It caresses my hand and cradles my head before it goes.
Everyone knows I have seen it by the smile it leaves on my lips.
I stand half stunned, half believing I don't deserve it
And fully hoping it will call me again tomorrow.

TK

MUSIC MAN

I can hear it, you know
Your melodic murmurings that escape
Before you even finish your song
Your badus and bah-de-yahs run free
Before you want them to
And they're beautiful
As you scratch your head
You scratch out harmonies
That lace together pieces of the wounded world
The folds in the frown upon your brow
Curl to the form of peaceful notes
To a song of salvation
The tap taps of your pen upon the pad
Write the songs all hearts pray for
And they are proud of their composition
I walk by and caress your hand
And feel your tune within me
A brush of your lips glues your rhythm to my soul
But something new is happening
As we sway to the silence of a song
You are still creating
I play mine too
My beat inspires yours
And we become a symphony by ourselves
Playing at a volume that only we can hear
We are colored by the jealousy of the world
I close my eyes and listen
I thank you
For
Allowing me to be your audience

TK

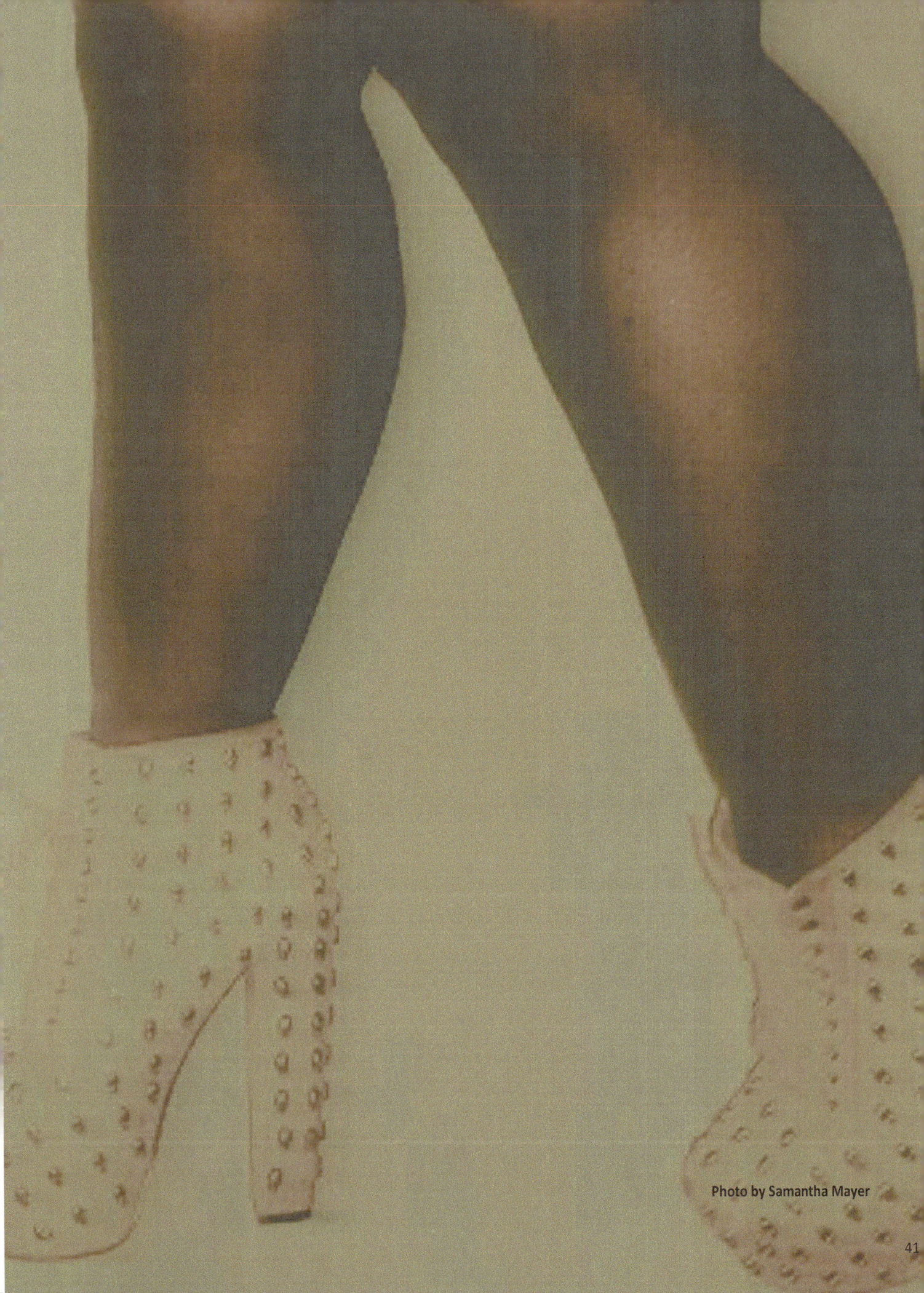
Photo by Samantha Mayer

LEGS

My legs are a treasure. But we haven't always been close. When I was little, Mama and Grandma would call them clubs or tree trunks. My feelings were a bit hurt, but that was before I knew what they meant. Clubs beat off unwanted things. Tree trunks are strong. Mama and G-Bird paid me high compliments. They recognized the parts of me that were strong and beautiful before I ever did. They made me agree to try and love those parts of myself. There was no way they could have known the way things would turn out. They never could have known that I would allow my heart to talk the strongest, most beautiful parts of me into opening up and let in He-Who-Was-Not-Worthy. Mama and G-Bird could not have known that I would give the most precious gifts a woman can give only to have them thrown back in my face. Like a dusty toy with a missing part, he left me in a corner and drummed it further into my head that he and I were going nowhere. And instead of using those precious clubs/ tree trunks of mine to sashay the other way, I let them weaken. As though my knees had done me the injustice instead of my foolish heart, I dropped to them and apologized for faults that were not mine and pleaded for him to stay. For years, I put wear and tear on the legs Mama and Grandma were trying to teach me to love. I bruised and blackened my knees making apologies I didn't have to and housed pains in my calves from running all over the world for him. And where were his legs? Somewhere kicked up, waiting for me to make an even bigger fool of myself. Well one day, these old legs got tired of running when *they* could have been somewhere kicked up resting. My knees got tired of being worn out on apologies when I could have been on them praying for myself. They got tired of being tired. So, I listened to these strong, beautiful, tree trunkish, clubbish legs of mine. I stretched them out until they remembered the strut I used to have before I met his sorry ass. When I was alone, they would dance up such joy that I could float on air for months. Oh, these legs used to bend, stretch and dance and make all the boys wonder what they had to do just for the privilege of standing next to them. Oh, how the boys would drool. Now they can break out those bibs again because I've got my legs back! And him? He can dream and drool over them too if he wants. In the new life of these legs—large like tree trunks, strong like clubs—they will oppose the Red Sea and never part for him. These legs are free. And we've got a lot of dancing to do.

TK

NAKED

Take off all your clothes and give them to me,
But not just the things you button up.
Give me what you allow to cover your heart.
Give me all the pains others gave you.
Let me dispose of them at will.
Give me all of the suspicions they have birthed.
Give me your inhibitions.
Give me the nights you only needed to be held
And no one stretched out their arms.
Give me all the days you needed to be kissed
And the desired lips had prior engagements.
Give me all the years you only needed to be loved
But your lover's heart was busy loving other things.
Give me the times you needed someone to listen
And she never lended an ear.
Give me all the hurt you've donned
Give me all your tears.
Take off all your clothes.
I want you naked for the rest of our lives.

TK

MY BODY

My body has never failed anyone but you.

When you are looking for someone to dress, my curves are too much for you.

I have too much midriff for that trendy top.

You want your garments to show a little leg, but never any as big as mine.

You want someone to walk your runways and while my strut is perfect,

Those legs aren't long enough for you.

You want someone for your magazines but my scars are too deep.

The ones that can't be airbrushed are unacceptable for you.

You reject my stretch marks and scoff at

Every extra minute poured into my hourglass figure.

But this body is dynamic.

It will be my children's first galaxy.

It will be the fertile land that yields life.

This body has been a jungle gym for nieces, nephews and little cousins.

Climbing its limbs has been their source of joy.

In this body, I feel the fullness and satisfaction of my own breath.

Feeling the tensions of my past fade away lets me know I am doing something right.

Sometimes this body is a little stiff in the morning

But I feel its vibrancy when it stretches towards the sky

And takes in the morning's air.

This body dances.

It moves through life with little to no effort and lets music fill every inch of it.

When I am in love, strong hands skirt around these same curves.

You know. The ones you can't dress.

They caress these legs that are too thick and short for you.

They run right over these scars you couldn't accept

So smoothly that I forget they ever happened.

All the extra minutes in this hourglass just become extra time to spend with me.

Every part you don't appreciate is a part of an ecosystem.

They are all here to radiate love and give a little bit of what it gives itself

To this the outside world.

So, my body might be a disappointment to you.

But it is a blessing I receive openly day after day.

TK

WHY COULDN'T YOU BE PRETTY?

Why couldn't you be pretty?
Look at all the other girls.
They don't have to beg men to love them and give them the world.

At your age, they're walking down the aisle.
All you do is pace back and forth
Saying "I hope he calls in a little while".

You have to take what you can get.
You don't have the freedom to choose.
You're not girlfriend material. You're just the one they use.

They flash their tiny midriffs
And end up set for life.
You'll make him a great new friend, but you'll never become his wife.

The only thing you can do is cry.
Things will never change.
Tears wash your face, but the rest of you remains.

Are your lips too big?
Do they not like the look in your eyes?
Or is it that they have a problem with the size of your butt and thighs.

Is your skin too dark?
Hair not long enough?
You want to say that's not what makes you, but everybody wants to be loved.

Maybe you're way too big-boned.
Maybe your shoulders are too wide.
Face it. They don't always take time to see what's on the inside.

You may be waiting forever.
You may not ever find "the one".
You may always end up crying when the day is done.

You'll just have to dream
And admire them from afar
While you bask in the sadness of being the lonely, ugly girl you are.

TK

SING

Sing.
Let a melody be the first thing to wake you.
Let it rest upon your heart all day.
Let it lull you to sleep each night.
When you speak,
Let the notes roll off your lips and soothe everyone around you.
When you're weary,
Lean upon the spaces between the staves.
When you're happy,
Tell it to the notes upon the page.
When you're angry,
Cry a piercing crescendo to the heavens.
When you're lonely,
Reach out and find a symphony of friendship.
Step lightly upon the keys of existence.
Choose carefully the tones of love.
Lay longingly upon the pitches of perfection.
Be free.
Be happy.
But, by all means, sing.

TK

Photo by Fredde Davis-Evans

THE NURSE

Her husband is dying. You wouldn't know it by looking at her, but he's definitely dying. He doesn't even know that she knows why. He doesn't think she's smart enough to realize that he got all nervous when the neighbor took sick. Before that, he and Paul had been best friends. And then after Paul's funeral, he shuffled back over to the house and took to the bed. Young girls from Missouri, or Misery as she likes to call it, aren't supposed to know about things like that.

The little bottom-of-a-shit-hole town she was supposed to affectionately call "home" robbed her of too many things she should have known. She was expected to be the thing some man used to channel frustrations and bring forth children but never truly love. And she was supposed to lovingly call him "husband". She was never supposed to notice that there was another race of working women that would have been glad to give her membership in their society if she would only get up the nerve to ask.

She was never supposed to notice that they hadn't made love in years and that when she dressed the kids for bed, she was doing so alone. She was never supposed to notice how he had suddenly taken an interest in "fishing". You know the kind with fishless waters and never a morsel brought home for the table? And *what* empty spot in the bed where her husband used to sleep? She was way too young and dumb to put any of this together. There was a lot she was never supposed to notice. He once said he loved her for all those things.

Once upon a time, she dreamed. As a child, she could sing like a lark and she knew that with her and her dreams, she was going places far beyond Misery. Why the hell did she *have* to go to Harper's General Store that day? As he helped her with her bags, she found herself amazed by his kindness. He was older but there was just something about him. He didn't frighten her the way her father had. He gave her the warmth no man ever could and she figured it must have been love. When he smiled his big, capped teeth, borderline geriatric smile, she felt safe. This was all her daddy's fault. Her daddy would be proud of the man he became though. "You stupid whore" and a slap across the face one minute and "You're so pretty" and a hand up her skirt the next. The stink of stale beer and cigarettes in her face while the pain of a world she was much too young to understand pressed deep within her. Each thrust just created another emotional hassle she would have to take a pill for later.

Ahhhh, the pills. Those little beauties made all the world go away. What would she ever do without them? When Sarah came home pregnant and Jimmie didn't come home at all, they were there to say "It's all right. You did the best you could". When she looked at Jacob and Annabelle as they slept, the pills said, "Stay calm. They will be fine. They will never turn out like the others". The pills talked to her when her husband wouldn't.

At first, he kept up the charade. He would come home late at night and climb on top of her with smells that reminded her of her father. There was something else that for the first two years, she couldn't pinpoint. As he treated her body like the last place on earth he wanted to be, she smelled something they didn't keep in the house. Thanks to her daddy, she had smelled it before. Old Spice.

It seemed he always had other places to be. He must have found the time to visit those places each time she was in labor. He was never present for the joy of the first breath or first cry. Just gave her a present days later as he would each young child days after their actual birthday. A seemingly apathetic "Good job, Kiddo" and a pat on the back that chilled her to the bone. The hand she squeezed was never his and he never wiped the sweat from her brow.

Sweat. That is all she seems to do nowadays. She lives at the bottom of a bottle and she has soaked through her clothes by the time she can make it there. She breaks her back cooking, cleaning, caring for the little ones, worrying about the big ones, changing adult diapers, giving medications, taking medication (at least his illness has one perk), drinking, giving excuses like "Jim's not feeling well today" and "The doctor thinks it may be a virus" with half-hearted smiles and lugging his fading, adulterous 75 pound frame from bed to chair, chair to bed, bed to chair, chair to bed…..to chair…..to bed…to chair….to…

Her husband is dying. You wouldn't know it by looking her. But she's dying too.

TK

HOMEBOY

When he speaks, I am reminded of home.
He carries cane fields in his greetings
And after the words flow from his lips,
They leave enough sugar for me to taste in his kiss.
Broad shoulders, bowed legs
And regal height-
Everything about him whispers strength.
But his eyes are reservoirs of gentleness
That I like to think he saves just for me.
I'm pretty sure God put those dimples there
For me too.
They remind me of the ditches near my grandma's house
Dug deep and perfect for hiding in
Until YOU choose to be found.
His skin is the color of the caramels
My cousins and I shared on the front porch.
We anxiously ripped off wrappers in
Anticipation of the saccharinity within.
His arms are like the thick
Quilts G-Bird made.
They could protect us from the cold and any monsters
In our dreams.
No matter what, they always kept us safe.
His chest is strong like that big tree near the driveway.
I can use it as home base during a game of tag
Or a place for shade when the sun is high.
His scent wraps 'round my nostrils
Like the sweet smell of Mama's strawberry shortcake
And lingers long after I have had the last slice of him.
Every time he looks at me, I get that same feeling
I used to get from taking that first sip of Auntie's lemonade
After runnin' 'round in the hot sun all day.
Every time he gets near me, I understand what the great-aunties
Were talking about when they told us about their hot flashes.
I wanna fan my coattails like they did
And let the sweet breeze blow through.
Every time he leaves me, it's like going back to school
And having to leave behind a sweet summer.
I sit and wait,
Head in hands,
Anxious just to get back there.

TK

'TIL DEATH: A ONE-WOMAN DECEPTION

(Curtain opens. A lady in a wedding dress sits staring at herself in a vanity mirror. She looks to be about 25. She rehearses smiles for a second, folds her hands, gives a genuine smile and begins speaking to herself. This character can be of any ethnicity.)

Lady: You're here, Baby Girl. You never thought you'd make it, but you did. Through everyone's doubts and all his baby mama drama, he chose you. In just an hour, you'll be a married woman. Hmph! It's a good thing too 'cause you aren't getting any younger. "Almost thirty" wasn't your plan when it came to when to get married. But you're still glad this day has come. You look good too. Cheryl said you were wrinkling early, but Baby Sister always has something to say. The only thing that matters is what *he* says though. And every single day for the last five years, he has called you nothing less than gorgeous. Okay, maybe beautiful a time or two. But who's counting? (*laughs*)

(She keeps smiling and primps mockingly. Slowly, her smile fades. The hand behind her head slides down and lays upon her chest. She looks sad and hyperventilates briefly.)

But will he still think you're gorgeous after he finds out what's been wrong with you? Will you still be his queen if you tell him? I mean, what if you're…..

(She gets up and fidgets and paces around the room. As she walks, she fights back tears. She shakes her head in anger with herself.)

No! No! Don't even think that way! It's your wedding day and today all things are positive. But all things are also possible. What if he leaves you?! And at the altar, no less! (*pauses*) Well, it's not like it wouldn't be well-deserved. Old and alone is what you always thought you would be anyway. (*Smirks*) If that happens, it will be the first time you ever get what you deserve. What if this is the big "I told you so" moment? Ugh! Get a grip! Get…..a….GRIP! (*shakes her head hard*)

(*Clears throat and takes a deep breath. Smile returns*) He loves you. He says so all the time. Shows it too. Yup. You love him and he loves you. It never fails. You always have to repeat that to yourself a few times before it sounds right. He loves you. He loves you. He loves you. (*Laughs hysterically, grabs her hair and shakes her head rapidly*) He loves you! He loves you! He loves you! He loves you! He loves you! He loves you! (*smile turns to anger*) Ugh! Just Stop! How could he love you?! You're a whore! No one loves a whore! He'd be out the door if he knew about all the men you've been with! And wait 'til you tell him about you and his brother! You're done!

(*Takes a deep breath, fixes her hair and smiles again*) But that was a long time ago. It was way before you met him. There was no way you could have known you'd fall in love later. God bless Robert for pretending you two had never met and keeping it quiet all these years. If he had ratted you out, you would have had to kiss your happiness goodbye. Thanks, Rob. Good lookin' out, Bro. Now let's just hope none of the others showed up to blow the top off this day. There is no telling what they would say. There is no telling what everyone would say about you. But worst of all, there is no telling which of your "others" could be to blame for what is in this little envelope. You've opened lots of mail in your day. But this piece didn't go away when you tossed it into the trash. It haunted you until you went back to get it. And you did so just in time for him not to see it. He came bearing good news that day too. Don't you remember? It was the day of his promotion. He was aching to tell you outright, but he decided to wait for the right time. At dinner over your favorite bottle of champagne was it.

You ended up leaving the restaurant early that night to go home for a long night of congratulatory lovemaking. But what were you thinking? If you really loved him, you wouldn't have touched him. You knew you could have killed him. What if on that night, when the most joyous part of his life was to begin, you saw to it that the whole thing was over instead? (*sneers at herself in the mirror*) You are such a selfish bitch.

(*Smiles*) But not him. He's not selfish at all. He is always thinking of you. He's even thought to comment on the fact that your "diet" is working. When you told him about your plans to slim down to fit into your wedding gown, he was the first one to say it wasn't necessary and that you were perfect the way you were. And he has taken such good care of you through this "stomach virus" that conveniently popped up right before the wedding. If only he knew. But that's just him. My Mr. Thoughtful.

(*A light knock on the door*) They're calling for me (*fixes her makeup, smiles and pulls her veil over her face*). It's time to be happy. The rest of my life may be ruined. But there is NOTHING that is going to ruin this day.

(*Gets up and walks out to meet the wedding party. End scene.*)

TK

HOMEBOY REVISITED

I wrote poetry for you.
Boy, was I dumb.
I was right about you reminding me
Of home.
But I chose all the wrong parts.
It wasn't the sugar of cane fields
I tasted on your lips.
It was more like that bitter quinine-based
Cough syrup Mama had to give me
For that stubborn summer cold I had.
What was is called?
Oh yeah. 666.
Extremely appropriate since what
Was on your lips had to be the devil's nectar.
Your lies and avoidance must be to blame for the aftertaste.
I loved your broad shoulders, bowed legs
And regal height.
But now I know they were only there to distract
Me from your cloven hooves and the tracks they
Would leave in my mind.
Those dimples aren't like the ditches by
G-Bird's house at all.
They're more like those big, dirty potholes
We got stuck in that made you late for school.
That skin of yours that I once thought
Like caramels
Now show the scales you managed to hide.
I realize now that you never meant
For your arms to be blankets,
But that I should have felt them as
Snakelike coils that would tighten
Around me to punish me
When I found out about her.
You've become just as cunning as that rattler
G-Bird and I caught that day.
But I think I trusted him more than I could
Ever have trusted you.
If his venom had a scent,
Surely it would be a lot like yours.
The worst part is, you bit two women
At the same time.
She probably loves you and I could
Have gotten there eventually.
You lost yourself in all this and the thrill of tasting
Us both.
Even after the confrontation,
You snapped and bit with vigor.

What you fail to understand is that I could
Shake your world with one phone call.
But my horns are not as sharp and prevalent as yours,
So, I left it to karma.
When you feel the stark sting of her wrath,
The memory of me
Will dance its way across your mind.
And I rest well knowing this.

TK

MISS MABEL WATCHES TELEVISION

kill me how peoples what got evathang
gits on tv an' paten dey ain't got nethin' when dey
gits home it's food on dey table clothes on dey
back and dey lights
ain't bout ta' get turnt off
womens what ain't neva been ugly
black out dey teefs widen dey lips
and nap up dey hair best dey kin
know dey ain't foolin' nobody
dem sadditty folks trade dey
propa talk for some "ain't's" and "y'all's"
and spec' us ta thank dey know sum'
bout growin' up wit' no learnin'
folks what ain't neva hafta worry
sat dere an' holla when we know
it ain't nethin' but a ac' fuh da' picha camma all of
it jus' a mess
i turns it on but i always turns it off jus' as quick
fake folks on tv neva meant us real folks
no good no how

TK

Photo by TK Long

Photo by TK Long

LAND OF THE...

I'm dead in America. This is a country where women can murder their own children, cry a few crocodile tears on TV, take a short tour of prison and be out in time to spend Christmas with their families. This is a country where I could be shot through the heart by a maniac drunk with undue power and HE get sympathy because he claims he feared for the life that HE still has. This is a country where I can't leave my children alone with a babysitter without bearing witness to them being viciously beaten by someone I trusted to care for them. This is a country where joyful days and meaningful marathons are spattered with blood because sick, twisted souls decided a bomb belonged in the middle. I live in a country where I can't count on my children going to school and coming home alive and enriched without having to worry about some bully waiting for them around the corner. For what? Because they don't like their shirt, or their hair isn't the right color or because they "think they're better than everybody else". This is a country where black skin gets you blacklisted and where light skin can make you the white elephant and you're pretty much damned if you do and damned if you don't. You say that I have the right to life, liberty and the pursuit of happiness. But you can keep that bullshit. My time on death row began once I left the womb.

TK

NIGGER

You can call me a nigger under your breath,
But make sure that's where it stays.
I would hate to take off these heels and earrings
And act in a niggerish way.
You look at me and see black.
But you never notice my mind.
You fail to see that I am the best boss or friend
You could ever find.
I won't preach to you about slavery.
I'm not an authority because I wasn't there.
But just because I wasn't working in the field
Doesn't mean I don't care.
Sometimes it seems I want to be white
Or at least that's what you say.
But I'm here to let you know
It's a new time and a new day.
I'm Black.
And yeah I choose wear my hair straight.
If I'm sick,
It's not because of some bad chit'lins I ate.
Yes, I know how to skateboard.
Yes, I love country and rock 'n roll.
But that doesn't take any of the Black away from my soul.
I do mousse my hair.
I do articulate.
Occasionally better than you.
Is that what you hate?
I am a ballerina.
I enjoy a good opera too.
I do all the things you think lil' Black girls ain't suppose to do. My
brother's name isn't Jamaal
I don't know "Pookie 'nem".
When I have to work at eleven,
I'm in at half past ten.
I'm not on welfare.
I don't have any kids.
My parents went to the same school
Your mother and father did.
I can drink from your water fountains
I can use the bathroom down the hall.
I have a lot of white friends.

But, oh wait! That's not all!
I can date your men now, too.
Lord knows they love my Black skin.
They've all dreamed of a touch of coffee
Every now and then.
I know my way around a pool
And I don't use butter in everything I eat.
I don't touch pork.
Hell, I barely even eat meat.
I can be Catholic if I want.
Sunday, I may sit next to you in church.
Then I may be the one you report to
Monday morning at work.
This isn't the Amistad.
You don't have a whip.
So I suggest you keep a tight hold
On those loose lips.
Because I have so much power,
This time, I'll look the other way.
This strong Black woman
Won't let you make her act like a nigger today.

TK

FRUITLESS

My tongue is not a garden for scripts.
It will never be that place that nurtures everything
You want me to say.
It is not the place where I keep everything all lined
Up in pretty little rows and nothing ever gets out of line.
When you think my words aren't pretty enough,
I still won't be a breeding ground for your propaganda.
I will never allow you to grow your fear and avoidance
Within my strong foundation.
I would rather burn the land.

TK

FAMILY TREE

I am Zora's daughter. She didn't know it, but she took my soul with her as she gathered her stories. My ear remained rapt as she taught me dialect and put a piece of me within Janie. Auntie Alice taught me my burden. She showed me the contrasts of strong Black women versus those who are broken and let me know what they were doing to my sisters in Africa. Great-Aunt Maya showed me that the arch I carry in my back was not flawed, but "phenomenal" and gave me answers to life's hard questions that roll off my tongue like honey and fly like sweet daggers into the hearts of those who oppress me. My cousin Sonia came up right behind her and put music in my womanly words that helped me to dance my way out of oblivion. Auntie Nikki gave me the chip on my shoulder and the courage to admit that I would rather walk "with the thugs than the people who are complaining about them". Uncle Bruce and Cousin Audre made me a femme fatale by letting me step into the center of the fight and see the rainbow in all its colors. I could better do this with the tongue Uncle Amiri helped me sharpened when people set off bombs and placed the blame on others. He taught me the power of "poems that kill". Cousin Langston let me run beside him and bask in the gleam of the river that is me and see the power of my dreams in its reflections. Uncle Jean taught me that no matter how bright that reflection, it was what my soul was sewn to that determined my identity. He helped me to discover that Lost Generation. Great-Uncles Paul and Claude's souls smile down on me as I talk about MY *America*, find kindred spirits and belt out a poetic love song as an ode to us as "a smile go flittin' by". Oh, but Great Aunt Gwendolyn showed me how to compose myself and bring back the bounce in my step while hiding the happiness deep within my heart. "We real cool" she said and gave me back my mystery. It is because my blood runs strongly this way that I do not hang my head, but raise it and puff out my chest. I strike fear in hearts one moment, but in the next, swaddle them like babes to my breast. They have given me the gift of the precious dichotomy of sweet mother and strict disciplinarian because they knew I was strong enough to bear it. It is because of them that I can go from howling hooker to well-rounded wife through my words and still be respected in the morning. Our family tree stands strong in its field as the winds of change blow. We do not apologize for the sway of our branches but acknowledge how bountiful the land is just because we stand on it. We let the earth write thank you notes that fall at our feet like bright leaves. The universe dances for us and we can change the song whenever we choose.

TK

Photo by Dan Hogman

Photo by TK Long

THE HAUNTING OF GEORGE ZIMMERMAN

Good morning, George.
It doesn't look like you slept much last night.
I stayed here all night just to see if my face
Disturbed you any more than it did that day in court.
I thought you could benefit from knowing what
It really feels like to be the victim.
But you see, nothing I could ever do to you now will
Ever get me a trial.
You, your own judge and jury, made sure of that.
Instead of causing the pain you say I did that night,
All I want to do now is ask you a few questions.
Do you still hear the rain, George?
Do you still feel the soft drizzle that
At one point in your life, might have been welcomed
But is now as pleasant as a diseased insect buzzing in your ear?
Can you still hear me on the phone?
And does "creepy ass cracka" still offend you?
Does that cold steel in your hand still make
You feel like a man?
Or does something about it singe your skin?
When you introduce yourself to the tiny corner
Of the world that does not know you,
Do you ever get the urge to put the word "murderer"
After your name, even if it's just to see what it sounds like?
Do you still hear the judge reading your not guilty verdict?
Do you smile? Or is that overshadowed by how heavy
My blood feels on your hands?
Does that weight pull you down enough
To make you fall to your knees and beg God's forgiveness?
You seem to be above the law,
So are you above Him too?
Did you ever think of just admitting your fault?
Or did the words "I feared for my life" always sound like
A better option?
And I can't help noticing how much you've changed
From before we met.
Do you eat in hopes that food will smother and drown
Your screams of guilt?
Do you choose not to run because it reminds you
Of the way I had to run that night?
Do you beat and demean the women you claim to love

Because you don't have the heart to punish yourself?
Now that you've continued your crime spree
Long after your acquittal, do you know how
It feels to be young and acting out?
Or are you and your lawyers also saying your behavior
Is that of the young "punks" and "thugs" you seemed
To hate so much?
Do you wish you had my hoodie to hide your face now, George?
Do you wish you had just stayed in your car?
When you helped to bail out another murderer,
You said that minorities have to stick together.
I'm glad you feel that way, George.
For me, football practice is over.
There are no more parties.
There are no more video games.
There are no more holidays.
There is no more homework.
There is no high school graduation
And I will never a wife and kids to occupy my time.
You see, we *can* stick together, you and I.
Thanks to you, I have got nowhere to be.

TK

I WANTED TO WRITE YOU A THANK YOU NOTE

I wanted to write you a thank you note.
So I picked up a pen and paper,
Put one to the other
And it came out this way.
Thank you for taking me on journeys unknown.
Thank you for mental exploration.
Thank you for cradling my senses
And inviting me into submission.
Thank you for giving orgasms to my psyche
Before even laying a hand on my physique.
Thank you for making me say your name
Before our bodies even met.
Thank you for enveloping me with your eyes
And allowing yourself to be bathed in my undertow.
Thank you for letting the waves of my spirit
Crash upon the rocks of your being.
Thank you for loving all of me
And I do mean ALL of me.
I wanted to write you a thank you note.
So, I pick up a pen and paper.
I put one to the other
And it came out this way.

TK

CAREFUL, OR YOU'LL BE IN MY NEXT NOVEL

Keep talking.
Keep giving me more to say.
You'll be my creation
When I sit down to write today.
Make me fall in love with you
I'll write you into my wedding.
But, piss me off and I'll leave you
At the altar sweating.
Give my body kisses and tingles.
I'll write you into my bed.
Break my heart in enough places
And you just might end up dead.
Look at me the right way
And I'll write you into my heart.
But look at me the wrong way
And I'll tear your soul apart.
Treat me right and I'll write myself
As your best friend through whatever.
Treat me wrong and I'll write in
A disease you'll keep forever.
Be good to me and I'll protect you
From all danger and pain.
Mistreat me and I'll write off pieces of
Your mind til you go completely insane.
I can be your Grim Reaper or
I can trap your fate in a cage.
It's up to you how you choose to
Appear upon my page.
It's amazing what I can do
With a pen, some paper and an hour.
I write.
Therefore, I am
The one who holds the power.

TK

THE WHORE OF CORPORATE AMERICA

You keep asking me how I feel. Do you really wanna know? In a word, fucked. I feel like Corporate America keeps undressing me, laying me bare, entering me and thrusting violently until it has left every piece of my soul that was once intact a mangled mess of despair. The sad part about it is, it's been going on for quite some time and I am really just noticing it.

For the longest time, I have been America's whore—content to let it have its way with me and smear my lips a shiny red with its lacquer of lies and put on a happy face for company. We may call its sister Lady Liberty, but don't let that bitch fool you. She's a freak. The things she has done to me are unspeakable and I really should hate everything about her. Then I look at things like decent homes, cars, running water, voting and food to eat and I feel love for her and am running back to her for shelter. Corporate America waits in the wing. I am their bottom bitch.

There is but one dream I really have and that is to be able to pick up a pen and write myself into my own pretty little corner of the world. This is a corner where I can see whatever colors I please, decide whether it is day or night and walk around all day in nothing but a cloak of my creativity if I choose. I wouldn't have to worry about running out of money because talent would be the only currency in my world. And I would be rich.

But Corporate America says my dream is not allowed. It slaps me, dresses me to its liking and sends me out the door smelling like deceit and foolishness. It tricks me into thinking there is a purpose to all of the things it makes me do daily. It numbs the part of my tongue that speaks the truth and fills my mouth with "Yes ma'am", "No ma'am", "Yes, sir", "No, sir", "Sure, I'll come in on Saturday" and "Yes, I'll stay later". When I get home and take off this unsavory uniform, I feel those words sitting at the back of my throat like a heavy pile of sawdust and immediately feel cheap and tawdry. I cry enough unhappy tears to build myself a bed for the night. For a while, I drift back into my forbidden dream. But the alarm clock lets me know how little time I have for peace. Six a.m.

Gotta get back on the corner.

The streets are calling me.

TK

The worst job I have ever had was

_____

I hated/hate it because

_____
_____
_____
_____
_____
_____
_____
_____
_____
_____
_____
_____

THE WRONG ALICE

This is when I knew my day job was driving me insane.

Down…..down……down, down, down…..Every day I fall down this rabbit hole where nothing makes sense. Every day, I follow the little white rabbit in the waistcoat who is rushing everywhere but going nowhere at all. He is always "late for a very important date" that will obviously NEVER come. Every day, I have a conversation with Tweedle Dee and Tweedle Dum who are thick as thieves, but both treacherously wrong. Every day, I allow myself to choke on the fumes from The Caterpillar's pipe and let him get me wrapped up in circular conversation in which he says a lot only to convey very little. That damn Cheshire Cat is always smiling and popping up randomly in the middle of my quest to just get out. I am always invited to a tea party I have no desire to be at with the Mad Hatter laughing and causing an uproar while singing happy songs when there is nothing to be happy about. There's that March Hare joining him in all of his idiocy while trying to distract himself from his own neuroses. And that fuckin' Doormouse that always chimes in on the conversation but clams up when she finally gets the attention is ever-present. I don't want to drink. I don't want to sing. As a matter of fact, I DON'T want to celebrate my un-birthday or any other day here with you. Don't even get me started on that Red Queen who thinks the whole world revolves around her. What do you mean "Paint the roses red"? They grew in white, Bitch. So, leave them that way. You can yell "Off with her head" as much as you want. Little did you know, I fashioned a string of pearls and hung a cookie around my neck that yells with boisterous saccharinity "EAT ME!" So, there is nothing your daft card soldiers can do to harm me. The White Queen is supposed to be here to save the land, but she stays far away in her castle. When she sends her periodic addresses down to the commoners, I tune her out and go sing with the flowers. "In The Golden Afternoon" is where I wish I had stayed. Conversation on that bank with Dinah was much more lucid than any notion she has that her subjects should respect her. The trickery of that disappearing Cheshire Cat has taught me that sometimes you can't trust the things that seem to be on your side here. So as for the White Queen. I don't trust that skank either. And they all are trying to convince me to slay some Jabberwock when the truth of the matter is, I don't live here, so I don't really care what happens to their Wonderland. "We're all a little mad here", they say. Well, my madness was evident before I peeked into their dirty, slimy slippery spiral and fell in to their vacuum of senselessness. The clock on the wall ticks and tocks to mock me. I adopt the White Rabbit's psychosis as I sing to myself "I'm late! I'm late for a long overdue escape!" More and more rows and rows of dark, dank cube-shaped prisons seem to appear as I attempt to claw my way out. I will be glad when I can wake up from this awful dream and make my way back to reality.

TK

HURTS LIKE NEW SHOES

I'm not playing. I have been on this earth all these years and I finally know what love feels like. To sum it all it up, it hurts like new shoes. You know how it is when you go into a store and you find that pair of shoes you think is perfect. Oh and don't let them match an outfit you already have because you just might have a fit! You pay the price that is asked for them with a smile on your face even if that price is way too high and you might regret it later. You get them home, sit them next to that outfit and pat yourself on the back for a job well done. Now, you know when you tried them on at the store, they were a little tight. But you brought them home because you knew that if you wore them awhile, you could break them in and make it work. With that in mind, you slip into them and ignore that little pinch you feel at first. You just have to wear them awhile and they will fit like a glove. But what about when you have worn them for years and you still can't get rid of that pinch? What about those days just walking across the room makes you feel like those stunning, still new shoes of yours just might draw blood? Yeah, there are some days that are worse than others but you know you shouldn't still be feeling that pinch. Now, not to sound like Forrest Gump, but "I've worn lots of shoes". And if any of the "shoes" I have worn read this and get offended, then maybe they shouldn't have been in my closet or they just shouldn't be reading this. But back to our regularly scheduled program. Let's talk about some of the shoes I have worn.

My first and still very favorite pair of shoes, I like to call My Trainers. Now I was just learning to walk in love so I was still a little wobbly. My Trainers and I were inseparable. We saw everything and we felt like there was nothing we couldn't do together. They showed me all of my first adventures when it came to matters of the heart. And they were just that--my firsts. But My Trainers, you see, had no desire to grow. I had so many places I wanted to go and things I wanted to see and I had to put them down. Then I picked up some Runners. You know the types. They are the perfect shapes and perfect colors but they get close to you, let you fall in love with them and work up a good sweat and then their job is done. I have worn more pairs of Runners than I even care to speak of. I did change it up for a little while. I got myself a pair of Boots. You know, as in these-are-made-for-walkin'. That is exactly what I should have let them do too. Now when I say Boots, I don't mean the sexy, 5-inch high ones. I mean the low, borderline cowboy ones. I took them home because they looked innocent and I figured I could make them work. But I had no idea they would be so much work. I mean, I had to keep them clean, give them a box to lie in, paint them, polish them and the whole nine. Those damn boots became a full time job. But they were ungrateful. Imagine how angry I was when I found out those Boots, who had let themselves go (I mean shafts wouldn't stand straight more than ten minutes most of the time, were losing their shape, and never did anything more than lie around had been trying to slip underneath someone else's bed as I slept. I had to let them go. I didn't cry. It was my birthday, so hell I went window shopping! See, those old boots thought that because I told him about my old Clogs that came between the Runners and him, that he could take advantage. The Clogs are the dangerous ones. These leave bruises when they touch your body and if you aren't careful and say the right things, they can break bones. I did miss one pair on the list though. Backtracking a moment, I did have myself a pair of Slippers. Now Slippers are the comfortable ones you slip into after a long day. They are untouched by the weather outside and don't really get all that much action despite their proximity to the bedroom. My Slippers were sweet and never ceased to amaze me. But these Slippers I loved so well stepped outside with me one day and a neighbor saw them. As innocent as they were, they were lured away and we parted ways.

Bringing you up to speed, I'm into Stilettos now. You know, hot, sexy, fun, headturners that make you burn with desire at mere mention of them. But see, Stilettos don't commit. They don't want to spend their lives with you and frankly, the pain of having them on when they are pulling in all other directions becomes unbearable. Eventually, you have to let those go too. I feel myself slipping out of them though. And I know that even though it will be strange when we part, eventually I will get used to it and adjust. Once I take them off, it'll be a long time before I decide on another pair. Until I find myself a pair of Everyday Shoes, I will just run barefoot. I'll close my closet door and forget about the older shoes. I will run around pinchless. I will finally be free.

TK

TRUST FALL

Sometimes I like to close my eyes and pretend men are in love with me.
I always get the pretty ones without even trying.
All I have to do is be myself and the smart ones sit down next to me and ask me my thoughts.
I can walk in the way that I do and the chivalrous ones want to walk on the outside of me.
When I listen to the genres of music I like, they sweep me into their arms and spin me into moonlight.
When I watch movies, the ones with the strong chests pull me close and either let me cry or fall in love
But secretly hope I will do both.
The ones with the honest eyes tell me the truth of all they see, even if it hurts.
The ones with the strong hands and arms defend my honor against the ones who disrespect me.
At random times during the day, the affectionate ones tip my chin up and kiss my lips.
The expressive ones whisper in my ear and tell me I'm beautiful first thing in the morning.
With the ones who want to grow with me, I see all the world's wonders.
The ones who want to know me lie with me and look for my pieces in my poems.
The ones who trust me share their most intimate thoughts with me and willingly show me their fears.
The ones who really want to go places let me meet them at the end of the aisle.
The ones who are unafraid allow me to be all of me and dare to love every part.
Love never seems to make sense when my eyes are open.
So I would rather close my eyes and trust the fall.

TK

WHY I HATED GABRIELLE UNION AND WHAT SHE TAUGHT ME ABOUT MYSELF

I had never met her. So needless to say, she had never done anything to me. But years ago, I remember that I just did not like Gabrielle Union. There was nothing rational about the scorn. But I felt like I was justified in harboring it. If anyone ever asked me about it, I would make up something. "I don't like her nose." "I hate the way she talks". "She thinks she's all that". I would say anything that came to mind. One day, I found myself watching *The Brothers* alone for the first time. It wasn't that typical watch party I would have with my girls as we high-fived each other on how fine the men were and how we couldn't stand Gabrielle's "bony ass", as we so affectionately called her. It was a regular TK Day where I just sat around and watched movies to entertain myself. I was watching the scene where she was lying on the couch with her head in Morris Chestnut's lap. After I got past hating because she was so close to such a beautiful specimen, I looked at her. I mean, I REALLY looked at her. The way she had her hair pushed back from her face and even though I know she had on movie makeup, there was nothing glamorous about her in that scene. She looked like a regular person. She looked like someone who, if I really tried, I could call a friend. That shook me because I had spent so much time spewing venom at the screen when I saw her in a movie. I wasn't supposed to like her. I mean not even for a second. I flipped off my TV and like a kid waking up from a bad dream, I sat up in my bed hugging my knees and rocking back and forth for a moment. Because I am someone who always wants to explain my feelings to myself, I had to figure out exactly why I hated her. So, I turned on my computer and Googled her. First, I looked at pictures. I talked to myself the whole time. "You said you didn't like her nose. What's wrong with it?" My pride spoke up. "Well, it's. " I shook it off. There was nothing wrong with her nose. Absolutely nothing. My pride spoke up again. "Are her eyes too close together? That has to be it. You always feel weird about people whose eyes are too close together." No. Her eyes were fine too. Still, I felt like I really HAD to find something. I stared. Nothing. So, I found another picture. Stared. Nothing there. Saw one with her smiling. I never noticed that she had dimples before. I wish I had dimples. *Shut up, TK.* The more I looked, the more I started to notice things. Gabrielle's skin tone and mine were not that different from one another. Since the beginning of time, light skin was what was always known to be beautiful. But here she was, a brown girl, and people loved her. Men found her sexy. I went through some red carpet photos and realized she hadn't "looked stupid as hell" like I said she had when it was live. She was actually very fashionable. I ran across photos from her King Magazine spread (the one that should have REALLY made me hate her) and shocked myself beyond measure. On the cover, she posed innocently in a black bikini and even had that deer-caught-in-headlights look I'm sure we are all guilty of having at some point in our lives. The one with the flower in her hair didn't repulse me the way I initially thought it did and the word "slut" didn't cross my mind anymore when I saw the one of her cat-crawling in just her bottoms. The spread was tastefully done and she looked absolutely gorgeous. I looked back through the other photos. She smiled. And it shined. No matter how much I hated her from my tiny dorm room in Birmingham, Gabrielle Union STILL smiled. She was not affected one bit by the fact that I found every stupid reason I could not to like her. My feelings had no effect on her at all and there I was, sitting on my bed shuffling through photos like a madwoman trying to prove something to myself. But wait. It had to be in the videos. I went through YouTube video after YouTube video trying to figure out what I didn't like about the way this woman talked. Kristen said "It's like she talks around her teeth." Maybe that was it. Wait. What? What the hell does that even mean? Gabrielle Union was articulate and even in character, rarely ever used colloquailisms. While I was going through the videos, I asked myself the obvious question. Why the hell had I seen so many Gabrielle Union films? The truth about the whole thing was that this woman was amazingly talented and Hollywood knew it. She wasn't just walking onto the set and giving HERSELF the roles. She was getting hired because she was working hard and obviously working well. In the end, I found that there was nothing wrong with Gabrielle Monique Union. She was a beautiful, successful, hardworking brown girl. She was exactly what I should have been striving to be. "TK, you are a stupid, stupid bitch", I heard myself say. I took some time to think about the friends I surrounded myself with who helped me bash this woman. Later, I would let them in on my epiphany and they would answer "I still don't like her". That told me there was something about this beautiful, successful, hardworking brown girl that they never wanted to be. I realized I was on a much different path than they. That caused me to examine them in other situations and realize just how little value they added to my life. I became a Gabrielle Union fan and decided that I, too, would become a beautiful, successful, hardworking brown girl.

Fast-forwarding to the 2013 Essence Awards, as though she wasn't already looking gorgeous enough to not have to say a word, Gabrielle Union stunned me. As she accepted her *Fierce & Fearless Award*, she gave a speech that kicked me in the heart. There were parts of her speech that were funny, but the rest of it was just real beyond belief. She and I felt the EXACT same about reading Huck Finn in class. We both prayed that we didn't run across a "Nigger Jim". We both reveled in the gossip and "took joy in people's pain and tap danced on their misery". She spoke courageously about her failed marriage and her journey to live her truth. I got teary-eyed when she talked about not wanting to "function in dysfunction and misery" but really wanting to BE happy instead of pretending to be happy. She talked about how easy it was to commit to misery. She said "Real fierce and fearless women are truth-seekers...We stand up and use our voices for something other than self-promotion. Real fierce and fearless women celebrate and compliment other women and we recognize and embrace the notion that their shine in no way diminishes our light and that it actually makes our light shine brighter". I am not ashamed to say that I sat with tears streaming down my face because I was in disbelief that this woman for whom I had once felt so much contempt for no good reason at all knew exactly what was on my heart and had been the same type of mean girl that I was. She spoke with dignity about her pitfalls and carried herself with grace. The hardest type of person to be is one that learns from experience. It is always so easy to drown out the lessons with blame. But there she was in front of everyone telling us exactly what she had learned. I stood and cheered louder than probably anyone in that room when she left the stage. I learned that it was possible for someone who had experienced some of the same painful things I had to come out on the other side of it with a smile and that the only shame should come in not sharing what you've learned.

As if that speech wasn't enough, Gabby (I can call her that since we are friends in my head now, was cast to play Mary Jane Paul in *Being Mary Jane*, a brainchild of my SHEro Mara Brock Akil and Salim Akil. When I would talk to my friends about our positions in love and life, I would always compare us to beautiful houses with broken furniture. We are all the inspirations behind the pieces published in this book called "The Truth About Women". But in *Being Mary Jane,* I get to watch the story of one of those beautiful houses unfold without having to sustain any more damage in the process. First of all, my girl is a broadcast journalist who is at the top of the game. That does something for me because even as I still try to break into the world of print journalism, I still have people trying to talk me into broadcast. I have not yet conquered my horror of seeing myself on camera. But because on *TalkBack*, MJ says a lot of what I would say, I get to live through her. But looking further at the character, on the surface, she appears to have it all together. She stops at nothing to be there for her friends and her family. She gives very little care to her own real happiness but takes extra care to LOOK happy on the surface. She has bad luck in love, not the best luck with friends sometimes and evenand even though she is driven by her career, at the end of the day all she wants is a man who is truly hers to lover her and maybe a few hardheaded kids to yell "No", "Don't" and "Stop it" at when she comes home. As I watch Mary Jane go through things, some parts feel as though I am watching a demo reel of the movie of my own life. And the fact that sometimes she doesn't do what is right or smart or may make her parents proud lets me know that my mistakes are okay and that sometimes it does take more than one time for your heart to break before you really start to hear it crack. She may not have gotten the role in Scandal. But I, for one, am grateful because I really don't think anyone else could have brought this home for me the way Gabrielle does.

Just as all public relationships do, Gabrielle's relationship with Dwyane Wade has come under scrutiny too. From people calling her a homewrecker to singing their "I wouldn't" and "I can't believe she" songs when the world found out about Dwayne's youngest son. I will admit to initially looking a little wide-eyed at the fact that there was a young baby in the midst with another woman soon after Gabby and D.Wade announced their engagement. But I had to step back for a moment and let something my sister Kenisha said echo in my head. "I don't judge the dynamics of any relationship because I will never know what it takes to love that man". I thought to myself, 'This woman has shown her strength. She has shown her intelligence. She has shown her courage. And she has shown, above all, that she is not a damned fool. If she knows about this baby and has seen fit to still become Mrs. Dwyane Wade, then there has to be a whole helluva lot that we don't know. And the fact that we don't know says it is none of our business'. I love that they are in love. I love that they have fun together and despite how it looks to outsiders, I love the fact that she, his two older boys, the nephew he has adopted and the new baby are going to be a family. I hope she continues to walk so far in the opposite direction of the naysayers that their voices become faint whispers. I hope she has truly found the happiness she has always wanted To this day, the only real reason I found that I hated Gabrielle Union was because she was out there doing what I couldn't and doing what I dared. But by looking closer at the reasons I disliked her, I got to look deeper at and get to know myself. I got to finally become a beautiful, successful, hardworking brown girl. And I made a promise to myself to not stop chasing my dreams until this heart of mine gives out. Thank you Gabby for showing me that I can be fierce and fearless too.

TK

THE WAIT

I don't belong in here. I mean, these folks are crazy. You got one over there in the corner drooling all over herself and one sitting next to me talking to her son Mickey that's been dead five years. Sure, I sang a few raunchy songs and loved a few dumb men in my day. But when I look at these loonies, I got better sense than any psychiatrist I ever seen in my life. There is this one lady named Idella who look like she coulda probably been pretty twenty years ago. But now all she do is sit around and sing the same damn line from "The Thrill Is Gone" over and over again. All day long it's "You know you done me wrong and you gonna be sorry someday". There might have been a halfway decent story behind it, but she got on my nerves too bad for me to ask. They won't even let me have my smokes in here. Nurse Fat Lady say, "We wanna keep those lungs pink and healthy". Shit. What I care about my lungs when I'm dying in here with these nuts anyway. Edgar used to say, "A lil' cigarette ain't never hurt nobody. It's them fools what smoke 'em all the time with the problems." Truth be told, me and him both was them fools. But you always gotta be able to explain your own wrongdoing. Edgar, Edgar, Edgar. He was the prettiest of the pretty and the dumbest of the dumb. But I loved him, though.

Now, a girl's daddy is the one who 'sposed to warn her about the pretty, dumb ones. But I reckon since my daddy was pretty and dumb and didn't give two Mississippi goddamns about me, my mama and my sister when it came to them other floozies in the street, it wasn't much he could tell me about the likes of Edgar. A woman can't stay 'round but so long not being cared for. So my mama took Virginia and me and left. Ginny ain't never have the good sense to know that Daddy didn't mean her no good. She was dark just like him, pretty just like him and a fool just like him too. Wasn't long after we moved in with Granny and Pop-Pop that Ginny became a teenager. She started runnin' round wit' some of the pretty, dumb boys in the neighborhood and ended up gettin' herself killed by some old man's wife. Yeah. She been gone a long time now. But she still come see me sometimes.

That must be Nathaniel comin' 'round the corner. I declare, you smell him 'fo you see him. I know one of these nurses is 'sposed to be doin' the sponge baths, but I'm sure the stank will jump right up off him and kill one dead if they came near him. So, they just leave him alone. Poor soul don't even know how bad he smells. He just walks 'round here with them yellow teeth that ain't been brushed in years and a leg just as dead as his glass eye grinnin' and trying to talk to every woman he sees. He better not come over here today 'cause I just ain't in the mood. Naw, he ain't like my daddy and Edgar. He don't look like he was ever one of the pretty ones, but he could out-dumb any fella he come cross. Good. He gone over there to talk to Idella. Maybe she will change her tune and let him know the thrill ain't neva been there.

Thump. Thum thum thump. Thump. If Cressie tap that cane on this floor one more time, I might run over there and choke her with it! They tell me she was somebody back in the day. They say she come from money and used to wear some of the prettiest clothes you ever did see. I believe she had some long, pretty hair 'cause it looks might nice still. But all she ever do all day is tap that damn cane and yell out "Henryyyyyy! Henryyyyyy!" Henry was her husband, but you'd think he was the butler the way she yell for him to fetch her things. I reckon Henry decided to do somethin' for himself. So, he went on and died twenty years ago. He was liable to do anything to get away from Cressie.

Lord, when is somebody gon' tell Paulette this old one-eyed baby doll ain't her daughter Scarlett? All day long, she go on and on about how she gon' feed Scarlett soon and how she gotta bundle Scarlett up so she don't catch cold. Last week, she jumped on one of the nurses when they tried to take the baby from her while she took her medicine. I thought they would never get her hands from 'round that poor man's throat. Reckon it served him right for takin' Scarlett 'way from her though.

If Willie ask me one more time if I got a quarter, I might haul off and hit him. Even if everybody in this room said yes and handed him one, this ol' fool ain't got sense enough to know that he can't go nowhere to spend 'em. He keep tellin' the nurses he goin' to the store. They just laugh at him and call him crazy behind his back. Shit. Can you blame 'em?

I really wish Mamie would shut the hell up. All day long she just sit there wailin'. She don't say no real words. She just holler out every now and then moanin' and groanin'. The nurses ask her if she in pain. She don't answer. The moanin' just continue. The doctor come in to check her yesterday and she spit the biggest mouthful of saliva you ever did see right in his face. He just cleaned off his glasses and left. But I could tell he wanted to punch that hag square in her nose.

I told you these people was crazy. Then the nurses got the nerve to keep askin' me why I don't say nothin'. That's cause my mama always told me you don't dignify crazy wit' conversation. I'm ready to get the hell outta here now! Where the hell is Ginny?! She told me yesterday she was comin' to take me home today. I been waitin' here for six hours and this heffa ain't showed up yet. She better hurry up though. If I stay here one mo' minute with these fools, I just might go crazy too.

TK

TAKING BACK MY FREEDOM

Excuse me, Sir. I need to know what your return policy is. You see, somebody gave me this freedom and I don't think it's working right. Looking at the ingredients, I see so many additives and preservatives that I just know there have to be counter effects. There are so many "Buts'", "If onlys", "Only ifs", "You must haves" and "Not alloweds" to even see what the active ingredients are. I mean, have you read this label? There is one part of it that tells me that my best friend and I shouldn't be close just because her skin is a bit lighter. There is another part that tells me to tell my sister she is free to give her heart to whomever she wants as long as they have different sex organs. There is also something in there that says my brother can only be my brother if he can honestly say he is "African American or Black, Not Hispanic". I really don't think that belongs in there. And what about the part that says we have to go to different schools? I thought the manufacturers stopped using that ingredient when they created the new formula years ago. And what's up with this taste? It's like a mound of sawdust sprinkled with words unsaid for fear of prosecution. It leaves the mouth dry, longing for the cooling waters of peace. And you know that is difficult to digest.

What's that? Where's my receipt? Oh, I have it right here. But I warn you that it's itemized and it is long. You see, freedom is supposed to be a package deal. But instead everything in THIS freedom had its own price. Just to name a few items on it:

Dignity and Free Will $11,051,831

Hope $1,800,000

Education $1,973,000

Unity $1,896,000

Uncontested Love $2,010,000

Acceptance $1,231,093

Religion $9,011,000

Peace $80,219,090

Achievement of Greatness $4,041,968

Erasure of The Color Lines $1,965,000

True Freedom of Speech $2,021,065

Belief In Change $1,020,011

Regard for Human Life In Spite of $5,211,000

Sir, that is just giving you a quick rundown. There are still more items on this receipt and you see how much this freedom has cost me already. I know that it is necessary and that is why I want to return this batch and get a batch that actually works. You see, this one does none of what was mentioned on TV or in the newspapers. But the moment you give me some that does, I will be sure to sing your praises to all that I meet. Surely there is something you can do. After all the years of "Your money is no good here", there must be something you can do to get me some freedom that actually works. That smug smile on your face tells me that you know if you refuse, there is nothing I can do. But what you don't know is that even though this freedom has not worked for me, there are chemicals in my cabinet at home that have. It may take centuries, but what I will do is take this busted, bland, no good freedom into my lab with me and substitute ingredients that can give it fire and flavor. I will lay a taste upon it so sweet that my brothers and sisters from all around will be coming to pull up to the table. You see, I come to you today a dissatisfied customer. But the years have made me a fiery chemist who can put you out of business for good. Now you can help me find what I need now and lessen the blow or you can leave me standing in line with this heavy bag contemplating my revolution. The choice, Sir, is entirely yours.

TK

*11/5/1831: The Confession of Nat Turner; 1800s: The abolition of slavery; 1973: Roe v Wade; 1896: Plessy v Ferguson; 2010: The beginning of more rights being granted to the LGBT community; 12/31/1993: The murder of Brandon Teena; 9/11: The terrorist attacks at the Twin Towers; 8/2/1990: The Gulf War; 4/4/1968: Dr. Martin Luther King, Jr is assassinated; 1965: The Civil Rights Movement's prime; 2/21/1965: Malcolm X is assassinated; 1/2009: Barack Obama becomes the first African American to become President of the United States; 5/2/2011: Osama Bin Laden is located and killed

"It is our duty to fight for our freedom.
It is our duty to win.
We must love each other and support each other. We have nothing to lose but our chains."

-Assata Shakur

EXIT STAGE LEFT

The only reason I turn on my TV is to be with you. When I do that, all the other unimportant people in the world go away. All that exists is you and I. from the time I turn the remote in my hand and let the rubbery "On" meet my fingertips. The anxiety of a job I hate filled with people I hate more doesn't even matter anymore. Of course, I have the comfort of your eyes upon me from the walls of my cubicle all day. But it is nothing like having time alone with you and hearing you speak. Those horrible people around me may call me crazy or think I am weird for choosing to surround myself with you every day. They laugh, but it never makes me angry. Instead, I pity them for never having the connection with someone like I do with you. They're empty and that is by no fault of mine. I never have to wait for a man to validate me. I never need you to tell me I'm pretty, since you are always consistent. The scene I am watching you in now is one of my favorites. I really don't mind the woman there with you since it seems you are looking straight through her and out to me. Your eyes say to me, "This is not real. She is not real. She is only an actress and my heart belongs to you." No matter how many times I see you with the different pretty faces, your eyes always send me the same message. So, let them go home and cry because they never feel loved or pretty enough or secure in their relationships. I don't envy them. At one point in my life, I was one of them. I waited for John to tell me I was beautiful and that he would never leave. But I never heard the words and I woke up one morning to find myself alone. But I found you and all the tears dried and the heartache ended. I have no desire to go back to the way I was before. On cold nights, it feels good to lie down with warm thoughts of you. And if I want, I can close my eyes and listen really hard and hear your sweet voice whispering my name. I sleep like a baby rather than crying like one. Tonight is a cold night, but it is a special one as well. Tonight, in celebration of your newest project, you are attending a premier that is happening only minutes from me. Sure, Hollywood was no place for me when I was that miserable woman from Connecticut. But now that I am a single, vibrant woman of the ages who is preparing to be your wife, the move and the ongoing money problems seem nothing less than ingenious. I know that green is your favorite color, so you will love the gown I bought for the evening. While everyone else is there all proper in their black and white, I will stand out like an emerald angel. I decided to wear my hair up because my mother always told me that made my face glow. And I cannot possibly be too bright for you tonight. After weeks of planning, I will finally see you up close. I laid eyes on you once in Virginia. I called out to you, but my love for you had not yet grown enough for you to have recognized my voice. By now, I'd like to think that as much as my heart has reached out to yours, they will get on like old friends. The event is flooded with paparazzi hoping to get a glimpse of you. They have no idea that your eyes will be focused solely on me. But standing side by side, we will make for a great photograph. So, I don't mind the camera flashes. I watch as all the people that I'm sure are somebodies in somebody's world move down the red carpet all too slowly for my taste. Your limo arrives and my heart starts pounding through my chest. I adjust my jewelry and get into the stance I have practiced in the mirror for weeks. Cameras begin to flash and the chatter grows louder before you even step out onto the carpet. When you are finally in full view, I let my eyes travel up your body as I always said I would. Your long legs, bowed at the knees and strong, reflect your years in sports uniforms. What I knew to be washboard abs hide beneath you bright white tuxedo shirt. Your red bowtie is the perfect lead up to the charming face that I knew was bearded a week before when you were spotted by the press on an outing to buy a Mother's Day present for your mom Katherine, with whom you are quite close. But now I can see the perfect skin the beard obscured from view and it only makes your hazel eyes blaze brighter. Your hair is much shorter than I recall, but it is a welcomed change. The crowd clamors, fully expecting you to proceed down the carpet. But instead you reach back toward the car. A slender, perfectly manicured hand reaches out and grasps yours.

The hand soon announces that it has a slender, perfect body to match. The crowd gasps and paparazzi trample one another to get closer to you. I stand still and cannot even muster a breath. There before me, in my spot next to you, stands the girl from the TV screen. Even though she didn't take care to wear your favorite color, you seem to be just as attracted to her in blue. Just as the photogs think they have caught something steamy, you sweep your little Barbie doll into your arms and plant a kiss on her that puts all the scripted ones to shame. The cheers grow. I feel my ears stop up. The earth starts to spin and I hit the ground with a thud.

"Some old lady fainted. You okay Miss?"

He called me "Miss". What the hell is his problem? Then again, maybe it's not his problem. Maybe it's mine. I don't look young and pretty enough to be on your arm tonight. Still, he can't be speaking to me. "Miss"? I can't make it worse by letting him help me up. I have to tell him I'm fine. And no matter how blurry my vision, I have to get up on my own and make it home. I pull away from him so hard on my way off the ground that I almost meet the pavement again. I look up to see you looking back at me. FINALLY, our eyes meet. But rather than the look of love I always thought you'd have or the look of desire I hoped you'd have when you saw me in all of my emerald green glory, you look at me in much the same way that a stranger would look at a child after they have fallen in the grocery store. Your brow is furled in concern, but after she tugs at your elbow, you give a nod and hold out your hand in my direction briefly. With that, you walk away. All the cameras turn back to you as you make your way into the venue. Pretty soon, I am left alone under the awning as the chatter of the crowd moves like a wave rushing in the opposite direction.

....

I have driven this street many times, but never have I noticed how lonely and mocking it is. My ripped dress, broken heel I had not noticed and I make our way back to the car. As the door slams behind me, those around me likely take it as nothing more than the normal closing of a car door. But at this moment, I hear every door of my life slam and feel their wind in my face. Their voices come all at once. "You never fix yourself up anymore! This house is a mess! And do you even KNOW when we last had sex?!" John's yelling was louder than ever. "Mom, you are NEVER going to meet this guy! When are you going to learn that this is all in your head?! It's no wonder why Daddy left you! You are insane!" Oh, Kelly. I pray that no man ever breaks your heart the way they have mine. "I never bring any girls home to meet you because you are a total embarrassment! You're a disgrace!" Brad, I can only hope you don't still hate me. "Stop looking for the most attractive guy. You will be lucky if ANY man wants to marry you! Now where's my dinner?!" Way to set the example, Mom. "Are you eating AGAIN?! It's a wonder you can still find your mouth. It should be buried under that blubber you call your face by now. Ha! Ha! Ha!" Rest in hell, Dad. "Well, maybe you should talk to someone. I mean, you have developed a bit of an unhealthy love for this guy." Some best friend, Cheryl. Everybody just shut up! SHUT UP! Every red light seems to be mocking me tonight. Does the whole world have to get a good look at my disheveled hair and running mascara? Or maybe it's the thick coating of shame you want them to get a load of. That HAS to be why you're making my drive home much longer than ever. On top of that, some asshole parked in my space and the lock that I'm sure a part of the small fortune I pay per month goes to is suddenly too good for the key that I know fits it. Look at this place. I draped it all in green as a tribute to you. The truth is, I don't even like green. The color of puss, infection, vomit and raw sewage. Only psychos love green. And what about these obnoxious paintings of you?! I have more pictures of you in here than I do my own family. It's no wonder they aren't here now. I loved you more than them. And the worst part is that I am only almost embarrassed to say so. Even though you turned out to be a jerk too, I still feel more devotion to you than I ever did John. Does that make me sick? Well, at least I am admitting it. And that is the first step to recovery, right? I think this calls for a drink! Let's see. Jim. Jack. Johnny. Oh, I never could choose my favorite amongst you. So, why don't you all come sit with me.

Yes, sit with me on this couch covered in an uninterrupted shade of puke green. You know, the more I look at you, the more I notice how beady your eyes are. That's definitely not a quality that shows strength in a man. Maybe a few drops of Ol' Jim will add some strength. A few? Who the hell am I kidding? Take the rest of the...bottle! Ha! Ha! I'm a better shot than I thought. Right between the beady little eyes! Jim surely is a sight for sore eyes. Get it? Sore EYES? Because that's where I hit…Oh, never mind. Jack is my favorite to hang out with. He is always that faithful friend with a strong shoulder to lean on in times of need. His truth burns my chest sometimes, but in the end, he always knows how to make me feel better. I'm glad he's here. If he wasn't, I would think what I am about to do was totally crazy. Crash! Bang! Crack! Clank! Yes, Jack! Thank you! I never realized these pictures were dreadful. I've never felt this strong. And it just feels so good to HIT something! Why didn't I do this a long time ago? Gimme that bottle! Let's get rid of some more useless shit. How about these DVDs? Who needs to see the same face a million times telling the same sappy love story with a different talentless girl each time? What was I thinking? Green curtains?! Well, not anymore! Ha! And who knew magazine clippings burned so well? I'm just learning all sorts of things tonight! Tiny little fires adorn the bedroom I once dreamed of sharing with you. I feel strong like an Indian priestess and they are my offerings. The more I dance around them, the more they grow and cast shadows across these forsaken walls. Tiny shards of light shoot out from them and bring a glow to the room.

The glow falls upon your face. Those eyes, beady and annoying to me a half hour ago, are now sweet and honest. And who wouldn't love that smile? It holds experience and innocence at the same time. But why do you have to look at me like that? Maybe the look you gave me tonight wasn't pity. Maybe it was an apology. I took too long to get to you. That has to be the reason you moved on with her. I'm so sorry. Johnny was always a sensitive soul. It has to be him that has me crying like a little bitch. It is so HOT in here! And this would be the night my balcony door is nearly impossible to open.

Damn….you…..sliding….glass….d-ahhhhhhh! Yes! Much better out here. Poor girl, maybe she just doesn't know. Maybe she has no idea that all she means to you is just a good time for now. She probably thinks this is forever. But I can't really blame her. After all, you don't appear to be telling her any differently. What did you do? Did you lie to her and tell her she was the only woman for you? Did you forget all about me as soon as you felt her body next to yours? Did you forget to even tell her my name? Where are my keys?! Since you didn't tell her, maybe I will. She deserves to know the truth. Or maybe going over there will make me look crazy. But what have I got to lose? Right now, I have nothing. No husband. No kids. And after spending most of my savings on this dress, hair, makeup and these shoes, I have no money. Maybe I was never meant to have you and just laying eyes on you in person was all the satisfaction I was meant to have. "A lady always knows when to leave" is what my mother always said. Maybe exiting stage left right now instead of trying to push on will make my life less of a tragedy. Maybe when I leave, you'll find joy in the fact that I loved you so much. The trouble is, these keys in my hand feel just as good as the air out here right now. I haven't decided if I am going to pay you a visit or hurl myself off this damn balcony. But either way, it'll be me or her. You have to choose. You WILL not have us both.

TK

My Celebrity Crush/Hall Pass is

_____

SINNERS GOT SOULS TOO
(AN ALICE WALKER INSPIRATION)

Brenda was incredible. had a heart of gold, a smile of diamonds, and the spirit of a saint. But in the end, the church despised her.

She came to the congregation of The New Canaan Baptist Church at the tender age of six. Her mother Emma used to dress her and her sister Lucy in ruffled dresses and socks and bring them to church regularly. I remember that Brenda would always be chewing on a wad of bubble gum, usually much too big for her mouth. Emma would chastise her and say, "I ain't raisin' no goats, Brenda Marie Carson. So, if you gon' chew like one, you might as well move to the field!" Lucy would laugh when her sister got fussed at, but because she was at least three years older than Brenda and still sucked her thumb, her mother would say, "And what you laughin' at, Sucklin' Pig?"

One day, Emma came up to me with a gum-chewing Brenda and a thumb-sucking Lucy in tow. She was a pretty lady of no more than thirty-five with troubled-looking smoky gray eyes, fair skin, and a rope of hair hanging from under her hat that extended to the small of her back. Emma was petite, good-natured, and received her fair share of whistles from the deacon's board. All we knew about her husband was that he was Creole like her and that we couldn't never count on seeing him at church.

"Pastuh Steel," she said to me, "I have wonderful news."

I placed my Bible on the pulpit and turned to see what her news was. Before I could even greet her, she began speaking.

"Both my babies have decided that they want to give their souls to Jesus! They want you to baptize them this Sunday." Then, she started preachin'. "They have decided that before they even begin to get caught up in this world of sin, they want to put on the whole armor of God and be washed, tried, true, and sanctified!" I looked to the back of the church for the ushers because I thought Emma was 'bout to have service all over again.

Always glad to see new souls come over on the Lord's side, I smiled. Brenda looked up at me with eyes just like her mama's. My heart melted at how pretty she was.

Just as I was about to smile again, she began chompin' on that gum just like Emma had told her not to. "Oh, Billie, spit that stuff out and talk to Pastuh Steel." Emma used to call Brenda "Billie", both after her favorite singer Billie Holliday and since she chewed just like him, also after her grandfather's pet goat. Brenda pulled the gum's wrapper from her little purse full of nothing but pennies and paper. She wrapped the gum in it and held it in her hand. "Passuh Steel," she said sweetly, "I wants to be baptized." She smiled and looked at her sister who stood next to her. "Me too," Lucy said with the hardest nod I had ever seen from a child. I loved to see young people happy about being Christians.

I had to sit down with the girls and carry on the normal conversation that took place after anybody decided they wanted to be baptized. I knew I would end up asking them the same questions in front of the congregation, but I began anyway. "Brenda, Lucy, so you believe Jesus died for the remission of your sins?" They both nodded. "And you've fully accepted him into your hearts?" They nodded again. "Well, that's just what me and the Lord like to hear." Just as I was about to get up, Brenda pulled on my coattail. "Passuh, Steel. I ain't believe in God at all at first." Lucy smacked her on the arm. "Shut up, Billie! Pastuh Steel don't wanna hear dat!" Brenda totally ignored her sister. "Mama kept tellin' me that God was everywhere and that he was always lookin' at me. I was thankin' that God gotta be pretty big if he can watch me and Piggy and be down the road watchin' our friend Suzy and her sista too. Then she told me that God was what make us happy. I figger since more than one person can be happy at one time, God really could be in more than one place at a time. So that means He gotsta be real." I had to laugh. If old folks understood God half as well as that baby explained him to me, we would be livin' in a world of alright. "That's right, Brenda. Every time you feel joy down deep in yo' heart, that's God talkin' to ya'. He give us everythang good in life." She seemed satisfied. She smiled, gave me a big hug and jumped up from the pew. I knew God had just gained one of his strongest soldiers.

That Sunday morning at the river, songs of worship rang out all over Georgia. Emma, her sister May Alice, her sister Shirley, her brother Bo, her brother James, her cousin Lula, her aunt Stella, her Uncle Willie, and just about everybody else you could think of came to see Brenda and Lucy get "washed in the blood". I read from The Book, struck up a hymn, and dipped the girls one by one for The Father, The Son, and The Holy Ghost. Everybody cried, sang, hugged, and shouted. That is, everybody 'cept the girls. Instead of joining in with the chorus of "I Know I Been Changed", they stood still and beamed at the crowd of worshippers. "Piggy," I heard Brenda say to Lucy, "We love Jesus, but we ain't never gon' act like that." I couldn't hold my laughter. When she heard me crack up, Brenda looked up at me. She held out her tiny hand for me to shake and said, "Pastuh Steel, I feel joy in my heart right now. Thank you for showing me where God was."

Now, my heart was good and full after the baptism and I reckon everybody else's was too because I ain't never had that many witnesses to anything that come out of my mouth before. They was in the aisles kicking off they shoes and everything. The spirit was movin'. After I preached my sermon on The Book of Revelation, I asked for a song from the choir. Mr. Otis played a little tune on the piano and Brenda got up and stood at the front of the choir stand. Everybody smiled and clapped and talked about how cute she was. But they didn't know that what was 'bout to come out of this child's mouth wasn't nothing cute at all. That baby had something to sing about and she wasn't shame at all. I guess because everybody wanted to know what she was gon' sing, nobody paid attention to the last few off notes Mr. Otis played before she opened her mouth. She began to sing.

As I let my, my mind roll back

To a lil' wooden church

Sittin' by the railroad tracks,

Just a lil' shabby ol' place

where we used to sing Amazin' Grace.

Talkin' 'bout a good time.

Oh, My Lord,

A mighty mighty good time.

Sista Josephine, one of the mothers of the church who hardly left her seat unless service was over, stood up and waved her handkerchief. "You betta' let Him use ya', Chile," she snapped.

By the time Brenda got to the end of the second verse, Mr. Otis had stopped playing and half the church was on its feet. When she sang, "Now very little money was raised, but many many souls were saved," Sista Alice hollered out from the back of the church and went dancin' in the aisle. Brotha Willie followed close behind her feeling the spirit in his own feet. The ushers ran from every corner of the church, but had a hard time holdin' it together themselves. When Brenda hit "Take me to the water," one of the ushers, Sista Alice's daughter Effie, hollered out and went runnin' by the altar. Some of the deacons had to come help with all that God was doin' that mornin'. Things didn't get no better when Brenda got through because Lucy came right behind her with "Father I Stretch My Hand to Thee" and ripped he doors off the church again.

The Lord knew what he was doin' with these two souls. After service, I went to talk to Brenda.

"Baby, you opened yo' mouth and sung that song like you had been doin' it for years. You wuttin' shame at all, was you?"

Just like the little woman she was, she said, "Well, Passuh Steel, if God give you something to say, you ain't got no reason to be shamed when He tell you to do it. My mama say it ain't nothin' nobody can say to you that God can't protect you from."

"Well, yo' mama is right smart. She right smart indeed."

"I know," she said, "That's how come me and Piggy so smart."

I smiled, shook my head and watched her run toward her mama and sister and grab their hands. When they walked out of the sanctuary, I looked up toward the steeple.

"You got somethin', Lord. You really got somethin'."

In the years to come, the girls anointed our choir with their beautiful voices and led Sunday school lessons. They were all about doing God's work. They spoke with wisdom beyond their years and were pillars in the community. Every time we went to deliver clothes to the needy or food to some of our members who couldn't make it to church, even if I didn't see anybody else, I knew I was gon' see Brenda and Lucy. Little by little Emma stopped coming to church. Thinking she was sick, the church members offered to take over some food and even some home remedies they thought would work. Now, I knew some of them just wanted to go over there to be nosey and find out why Emma had stopped coming to church. But part of me didn't mind because I wanted to know for myself. We would ask the girls where they mama was and they would always say she was at home doin' the wash or she was out of town visiting with her family or something. Then when we would go after church to try and sit with her, nobody would ever answer the door. After a while, I just left it alone and made myself content with just prayin' for her.

Even though both of them could sing, Brenda was a might better at it than Lucy was. But somethin' in my heart told me that Lucy had been called to preach The Word. Folks in the church looked down on women who said they was called, but I ain't never thought God saw fit to keep no woman from tellin' nobody how good He is. But I ain't one to keep up mess, so we never did talk to loud about it.

One day during a church picnic, Brenda and Lucy sat under a shade tree singin' to some of the younger children. Sista Johnson poured bowls full of her famous chili. Deacon Thomas lied about how "pretty" he was back in the day and Brotha Jones whistled at women and played cards.

Everybody was just havin' a good time. In the height of our merry-making, we heard a woman cryin' across the field. I look toward the voice and see May Alice running toward the picnic.

"Ohhhhhhhhh, Passuh," she cried as she grew closer, "Ohhhhhhhh Passuh, he done killed her!" As she reached where I was standing, the robust woman fell into my arms, almost knocking me over. "Now, May Alice," I said, "calm down some of that cryin' and tell me what's wrong with you." My shirt was already wet with her tears.

She stood up and tried to stifle her sobbing. The congregation gathered around the two of us. May Alice sniffed and sobbed, "That devil done killed my sister!" She fell on me again. "May," I said, "What John done did to Shirley?" She shook her head hard, "I don't reckon John dunt nothin' to Shirley, Passuh. But dat heathen Junior done dunt somethin' awful bad!" Everybody waited for her to finish talkin'. "She gone," he said, "He done killed my sista! He done killed Emma!" Everybody started cryin' at once and hugged May Alice. It felt like a hole was inside me. Not all the baked beans, chicken, and peach cobbler in the world could have filled that up. They tried to comfort the children, but there was no use. Brenda took it the hardest. She cried until she was hoarse and fainted. She had been closest to her mama, being the baby and all. And the child looked so much like her that for most of her life the members of the church called her "Baby Emma".

Nobody ever found Junior Carson. Some folks say he skipped town and bought him and his girlfriend a house in New York with Emma's money. But the truth is, don't nobody know where he went right after he left Georgia. After seeing Brenda's bruised body and all her broken bones, we can all be sure that he restin' in hell now though. It seemed like folks was even sadder about what happened to the girls than they was about what happened to they mama, though. Brenda and Lucy got sent to St. Louis to stay with Freda, Emma's oldest sister. The church wasn't happy about two young girls going to live with a lounge singer, but we all knew that none of us could provide for them the way Freda could. So, we shut our mouths and let them go.

****

I sat in my study talking to God before I was supposed to go deliver His word. I knew I was supposed to preach about the prodigal son because He came to me in a dream that I had had for three nights straight. I stood up, turned out the light, and went to lead His flock. The Spirit made itself known in the church that day. All through my sermon, a lady in blue caught my eye. Though I was sure I had never seen this woman before, she looked familiar to me. She had big gray eyes that seemed even brighter than her blue suit. He wore a subtle hat that certainly got more attention than some of the big ones in the room. Her face was covered in smooth skin and at first glance, she could have easily been mistaken for a white woman. Only occasionally offering an "Amen", she smiled and nodded her head throughout the entire sermon. I had seen that somewhere before.

After service, Sista Thomas came up to me with a concerned look on her face. "Pastuh Steel," she said, "I need to speak to you." I really hated to see Christine comin'. She always needed to speak to me and what she needed to speak to me about was barely ever somethin' that concerned her anyway. But like a good messenger of God, I said, "What is it, Sista" and prepared myself to listen. She came close to me as though she was sharing a secret. "Pastuh, we don't want *her* here." I looked around to find the person she was talking about. She yanked me down by the shoulder like I was about to get my head taken off by a 747. She must have known I was confused. "I know you saw her step up in here in that bright blue suit. She may as well had wore a red one. She's bathed in the blood of Jezebel anyway." I still had no idea what she was talking about.

"Christine, what you talkin' 'bout?!".

She pulled me ever closer and in breath that stank of stale chewing gum she said, "That is Brenda Carson over there! You know that singer who has been calling herself Candy Sweet! She the one that's been singin' in them clubs and makin' them sinnin' noises on them records! She the one been posin' wit' hardly no clothes on! She the one takin' them women's husbands! Now we can't call ourselves Christians and worship with the devil, too!"

I'm sure Christine kept talkin', but I didn't care what she was sayin'. I knew the woman in blue looked familiar for some reason! She had Emma's eyes and a body I had never seen before. But, I recognized the soul. Brenda had come home. I had no idea who Candy Sweet was, but the woman in blue was Lil' Brenda Carson.

I watched her out of the corner of my eye as she held Brotha Jackson's granddaughter in her lap and let the baby play with her long braid even though her hands was covered in sticky candy. She and the baby laughed and threw back they heads. Yep, that was Emma's chile alright.

It seemed like she knew I was thinkin' about her 'cause when I had that thought, she started walkin' toward me. Christine didn't like this. So, she shot her an evil look and swiftly walked the other way. Brenda smiled and extended her hand to me. She smelled like sweet potato pie fresh out the oven. Her hand was soft like cotton, but the heat I felt around my collar when I shook it was a might better than any heat I had done ever felt in a cotton field.

"Pastuh Steel," she said with a familiar smile, "I bet you don't even remember me." She spoke with her mother's Louisiana twang. Instead of shaking her hand, I said, "Brenda Marie Carson" and went to hug her. When I squeezed on to her, the smell of sweet potato pie got stronger and I reckon it wasn't just her hand that felt like cotton. I reckon it was all of her.

She pushed back, looked at me and said, "I'm surprised you recognized me. Folks been lookin' at me like a stranger all day long." I looked at her face. She looked even more like Emma than she ever had before. How could anybody look at this chile like a stranger?

We sat and talked about what she did when she left the picnic that day. She told me about how many questions her and Lucy had asked God. She told me about how mad they was when they didn't get no answer and how hard it was for the family to deal with 'em. Then she told me that Lucy had done married a doctor and that they had done bought two houses. She said that after church, she was gon' go over to fellowship with her and her husband and that I should come too. At first I didn't want to. I knew it was gon' feel strange to be the only old gray head sittin' in a room full of children. But, I went anyway.

****

By the look of Lucy's house, she had done married herself a *good* doctor. It was on the land that Sista Jenkins' house use to be on. But this house was ten times as big as Sista Jenkins' was. It was tan with brown shutters and looked to be three stories high. Two fine Buicks sat in the driveway and a little girl stood next to one of them, lookin' at me with wide eyes. I hadn't never been too good with children, but I bent down and talked to her anyway. "I'm lookin' for Brenda and Lucy," I said.

Louder than any grown woman I had ever heard, the chile yelled in my face, "Mamaaaaa! Auntee Billieeeeeeeee! Some man want y'all!"

I watched the child until she disappeared around the corner of the house. A woman came out onto the porch and put her hands on her hips.

"Emma, what are you yellin' about out here, Girl?! I done told you about all that!"

Her long black hair hung over her shoulders and even though the sun was in her eyes, I could see that they was gray. "Pastuh Steel," she said, "I am so glad you came. It has been a long time." The woman I knew to be Lucy came up to me and hugged me. She didn't smell like sweet potato pie, but more like a flower. She looked at me with weepy eyes and repeated, "It has been a long time." Before the fat tear fell from her eyes, she said, "Come on in here and get you somethin' t'eat." I followed her up the steps into the foyer (Now I ain't never have no foyer at my house. This is just what Lucy said it was called). When I walked into Lucy's living room, I felt like I was in a museum. She had art all over the walls and what looked to be antiques all over the tables and on shelves on the walls. Before my bottom jaw had the chance to hit the floor, Lucy appeared in front of me with a tall light-skinned man next to her.

"Pastuh Steel," she said, "This is my husband Dr. Jasper Cross." The giant stretched out his large hand to shake my much smaller one. In a deep, almost scary voice he said, "I have heard so much about you, Reverend Steel." Nobody had ever called me
"Reverend" before. When he said it, it didn't even make me feel like myself. But I smiled and said I was glad to meet him anyway.

I sat down on Lucy's butter soft leather couch and looked around. Lucy offered me coffee and she and Jasper came and sat down across from me. I had never seen two people look so pretty next to one another. They looked like they should have been in one of the paintings on the wall. Jasper had short, wavy hair that he parted on the left side. He wore a fine suit and shoes with gold on the tips. I found myself hoping he didn't get all dressed up on the 'count of me. He was thin, but he didn't look sickly like most skinny folks I knew. His jaw was strong and his hazel eyes blazed in his head like fire.

It turned out Jasper was from St. Louis and that his mother was from the same part of Louisiana as Emma was. Lucy joked and said they had to "ask questions and pray to God not to be kin" before they agreed to marry. He also had some convincing to do since while he reminded her of her mother, Jasper also carried her father's complexion. She wanted to get as far away from anything that reminded her of Junior as possible. After a few months of begging and pleading, he won her over. He had graduated from some medical school that I couldn't even pronounce and he was one of four boys. He met Lucy one night at a St. Louis nightclub and said that even if they went back today he was sure she would still be the prettiest thing in there. They seemed very much in love.

"I was sorry to hear about Sista Steel," Lucy said, "Brenda and me did love her like another mother." I nodded. It had been years since my wife passed and I tried to think about it as little as possible. The look on Lucy's face was like Alberta had died all over again.

Seeing this, Jasper said, "Speakin' of Brenda, where *is* that girl with that bunt cake?" On cue, Brenda came staggering into the house with more bags than she could handle. We all got up to help. After putting all of the groceries away, Lucy, Jasper, and me returned to the living room. Brenda stood in the kitchen drinking a glass of water. She wore a yellow dress and the rope of hair that once hung from her head was lying over her shoulders in big soft curls. Because her dress was so short, her shapely legs looked a lot longer. Just like she used to do when she was a little girl, she bounced into the living room to join us. She sat down next to Lucy and smiled at me.

"So, Pastuh Steel," she said, "You didn't have no trouble followin' my direction, didjuh?"

I laughed and said, "Girl, a arrow couldn't have shot no straighter! I came right here."

Looking satisfied with herself, she ran her fingers through her hair and said, "So, what you been up to all these years?" I couldn't help but think. I had asked myself the same thing, but never could get an answer. The truth was, my life had been pretty empty since Alberta passed.

But instead of looking disappointed, I just said, "Well, I just been tryin' to keep myself up and tell people what thus said the Lord. Ain't too much to be done other than that."

Lucy bowed her head, raised her right hand, and said "Amen, Preachuh".

Jasper nodded, but Brenda's eyes stayed fixed on me. She kept her same smile and said, "Well, you doin' a good job of keepin' yoself up. You look good." For a second, I though I saw her wink her eye at me. But I knew I had to be crazy. What would a pretty young thing like Brenda be tryin' to pitch woo at me for? The po' chile probably just had something in her eye. So, I didn't say nuthin'. I just kept talking.

"Ain't much to hear from an old man like me," I said, "What y'all been doin' up in St. Louis city life?" Like I remembered seeing her do when Sista Pearl asked her to sing "Jesus Loves Me" to the Sunday school class, Brenda perked up.

"Well," she said, "Me and Lucy didn't take to it at first. But when we met Sin it was all better." I must have looked crazy because Brenda and Lucy both laughed at me after they looked at me for a while. "Naw Pastuh," Lucy said, "It ain't quite like you thank. See, Aunt Freda left Uncle George and found herself a new boyfriend. His real name was Ralph Walker, but they called him Chicago Sin. He was from Chicago and they say he was black as sin." I laughed a little but I thought it was a shame for folks to talk about one 'notha like that. Brenda went on with her story.

"Aunt Freda and Sin started out hustlin' at a club called The Ice Box. They called it that 'cause that was where the coolest folks hung out at. She was a singer and he ran numbers. They liked the way things at The Box ran, but they wanted their own place. One day, Sin got lucky and come into his own. He come home and say, 'Baby, this is it! We gettin' our own joint!' And just like that, him and Aunt Freda packed up and moved me and Piggy to the other side of town. At first, we was mad 'cause we liked the old house and didn't wanna leave it. But Sin say he had bought us a bigger one where we could each have our own room if we wanted to. He say things was gon' be much better in East St. Louis. And good ol' Sin, he kep' his word, too. Him and Aunt Freda opened The Shuga Sack as soon as we got there. Since they ain't have nobody to watch us at home, me and Piggy always went to work wit' dem. We would sit 'round and listen to the girls tell stories 'bout they tricks and the boys talk about the fights they got into. Boy, we loved hearin' dem stories. Pretty soon, we all became like a big family. That was good for us since we ain't never meet much of our own family. We felt we had somethin' tuh belong tuh."

Listening to Brenda's story made me wish I was there. It seemed like she had seen more before she was ten than I did my whole life. I wished I could have been right there at The Shuga Sack, young and lookin' for life. Knowing that that wuttin' the way a man of God was s'posed to behave, I felt right shame of myself.

"We wasn't allowed to do much when we was young," Brenda started again, "But when we got older, Aunt Freda gave us the choice to sang, work the bar, or sell cigarettes. Now we had never heard tellin' of no woman behind no bar and we didn't care to be 'round no cigarettes. So, we started sanging at The Sack every night. Piggy was much more into her schoolin' than I was, so she quit and kep' up with her learnin'. I just couldn't stay away from that stage, though. Pretty soon, Freda give me the name Candy Sweet and made me her headliner. The rest, like folks say, is history."

"Well, Little Girl," I said folding my arms, "Is you got any records out?" Without saying nothing, Brenda got up and broke into a song and dance.

Boy, Oh Boy, why is yo' mouf hangin' down?

Boy, Oh Boy, why is yo' mouf hangin' down?

Is it cause ya' old lady got another boy that live uptown?

Boy, Oh Boy, now ya' know she ain't treatin' you right.

Boy, Oh Boy, now ya' know she ain't treatin' you right.

When she leave, come on by and I'll rock and roll ya' tonight.

Her voice was like bells. It was a far cry from the voice I could remember it being in her younger days, but it was still one of the most beautiful things I had ever heard. Though Brenda was young and she always looked wise and alive, she looked more alive still when she sang. It didn't even bother me none that that lil' girl I knew was singin'
'bout rockin' and rollin' somebody. Now I had been a preacher for years. But I had been a man even more years and that was just enough time to know exactly what that meant. But I didn't say nothin'.

I smiled a little. It still didn't feel quite right for me to be calling Lil' Brenda Carson no Candy Sweet. I could still see her wit' dem curly pigtails, skinned up knees and a whole pack of chewing gum in her mouth. Lil' Brenda. Lil' Billie. That's who she was to me. I thought better 'bout even mentioning anything 'bout her being called Candy Sweet. I knew that whatever reason Brenda had for puttin' on them lil' dresses and singin' all them sinful songs had to be a good one. I didn't really care so much what she was singin' about, long as she was still singin'. I made a mental note to myself to talk to the Lord about that on Brenda's behalf later. She was still usin' what he gave her and the fact that she was back in town said that she wasn't usin' it for those things no more. Maybe He wouldn't be so angry with her.

After a hefty dinner, Lucy sent her daughters into the other room to play while the grown folks talked. We all sat in the living room and talked until it was near dark outside. They told us all about the days at the Shuga Sack. I heard 'bout characters like Ol' Fool Brown, Mammy Red, and Smoke Eye McGee. But, Lucy and Brenda both got low when they talked about the day Aunt Freda died. "Look like I can still see her lookin' at me sayin' 'Take care of each other'," Lucy said. I remembered Freda being a sweet lady. It made me a might sad to hear that she wasn't on this earth no more. After we all sat there for a while, Jasper said, "Well, she in a better place now, though." Now even bein' a man of God and knowin' that we s'posed to have faith, I never understood why folks always say that when they don't know if a soul gone to heaven or hell. But I didn't argue none. I just nodded and said, "Lord knows she is." That seemed to cheer Brenda and Lucy up a little. I stood up and said, "Well, I have enjoyed visitin' with y'all. I 'preciate y'all asking me over. I don't get out the house much 'cept tuh go tuh da' church." Lucy stood up and took my hand. "Any time, Pastuh Steel." Now, people had said that to me before. But I really felt welcome that time. "I'll walk you to your car," Brenda said. I finished shaking hands with Jasper and Lucy and walked toward the front door.

Brenda was already standing near my car door. When I reached the bottom of the steps, she said, "Ya' know Pastuh Steel, I ain't stopped thinkin' 'bout the church since I left.

Y'all was more like my family than my own family itself. And if it's alright wit' you, I wanna get back in the choir. I wanna sang next Sunday." After hearing what Brenda's voice had become, I wanted to welcome her with open arms. But the Lord said that everything must be done rightly and in order.

So, I said, "Well, you know Sista Thomas is in charge of the choir. You would hafta talk to her and the rest of the members." Brenda nodded like a schoolgirl and leaned in to kiss me on the cheek. The smell of sweet potato pie filled my nostrils again and for that brief second, I was back home in my mama's kitchen. After my body cooled back down to regular temperature, I said goodnight and got in my car.

On the way home, me and God had a long talk. "Now I know I ain't s'posed to be feelin' nothin' bout that young woman", I said, "It ain't nothin' but lust. I ask that you forgive me Master and take away them impure thoughts." When I was pretty sure He had forgiven me, I just stayed quiet for the rest of the way home. I didn't realize how tired I was at Lucy's house, but all I wanted to do was put on my pajamas and go to bed. So, that's just what I did.

I could normally sleep pretty good, but not this night. I could see The Shuga Sack plain as day. I saw the cigarette girls, the purple walls Brenda talked about, the big table that Freda and Sin sat at, the regulars sprawled out drunk at the bar, and the gamblers playin' cards in the corner. I could smell the smoke and the liquor and I could taste the ribs on the plates. But the thing that delighted me the most was the fact that I could see Brenda onstage wearing a red dress with a flower in her hair. She sang a slow love song I didn't recognize and had a seductive look in her eye that was just as strange to me as her song. In the middle of the song, she stepped down from the stage and walked out into the audience. Men whooped and hollered as she walked by but she didn't pay 'em no mind. She just smiled and kept on singin'. She came close to me. I could feel myself sweating and shaking.

When she sang in my ear, it didn't sound like words at all. It sounded like she had the voice of the ocean and every time she moved her lips, a new wave was born. Her song washed over me and I didn't fight the tide none. I was swimming in the smell of Brenda's skin, swimming in the warmth of her breath on my neck. I was swimming and I was……trapped.

I woke up and found myself tangled in my sheets. I had done wrapped them around me like a straightjacket. For the thoughts I had just had about this woman, I felt like I really shoulda been in one. When I unwrapped myself, the sweat just poured off me onto the bed. "Lord, forgive me," I whispered.

My dreams continued all week long. When Saturday night came, I found myself praying the same prayer for God to take away my impure thoughts more than I was for the right message for his flock the next day. I didn't know how I was gon' get through my sermon with these thoughts running through my head. But lo and behold, Sunday morning came whether I knew what I was gon' do or not.

Brenda sat in her same spot only this time, she wore a yellow suit that complemented her skin perfectly. She was getting the same looks from the members of the congregation as she did her first Sunday back but she didn't care. She mouthed the words to every song the choir sang and got into the service anyway. I knew the message The Master had managed to lay upon my heart (in the midst of all that sinful mess) was the right one. When the choir finished singing, I took the pulpit.

"Church," I said, "this mornin' I wanna talk to you 'bout turning the other cheek." I don't know what it was but today, everybody whooped and hollered more than they had before. And I wasn't even in the middle of my message yet.

"Now, when I was a lil' boy growin' up in Mi'ssippi, me and my brother used to fight all the time. I used to always run cryin' and tellin' that Ray had slapped me. Mama would get both of us together and tell us that we could slap each other all we wanted to, but there wasn't nothin' that could compare to the blow God would strike on the 'count of us being mean-spirited. Mama said that when God slapped us, that was somethin' we couldn't get up from. But my brothas and my sistas, I'm here to tell you that you can slap your neighbor all you want, but when God slaps you back for slappin' them, there ain't no comin' back. My Bible says, 'Love thy neighbor'. Church, we are a family. At least we s'posed to be. I gotta say that there is less love in here than what is going on out there in the streets."

Half of them were on their feet shouting, "Go on, Preachuh" and clapping wildly. Now I had never questioned the smarts of my congregation. But they didn't have good sense enough to know that I was talkin' about Brenda turnin' the other cheek to them and that I was talkin' about them not showing Brenda no love. Them hypocrites said, "Amen" anyway. Rather than gettin' they goats on it, I left them to God and went on with my sermon.

Now, I'm not a betting man, but if I was, I woulda put everything I had on it that if they eyes coulda been knives, they'da killed Brenda that Sunday. But, she kept right on praisin' the Lord and didn't let them get to her none. The spirit ran through the church that day and if I may say so without seeming boastful, God allowed this ol' sinner to preach one of the best sermons he ever heard in his life.

After service, I shook hands with the deacons and talked to them about the new church buses. From the back of the church, I heard commotion. I heard Christine say,
"Who does this floozy think she is?! *Candy Sweet*. Hmmph! Ain't nothin' sweet about her." As soon as she said that, the entire deaconess board gathered 'round.

Brenda took off her hat and said, "All I did was ask if I could come back to the choir! You should be glad I'm askin'! I might be able to get rid of yo' ol' tone deaf directin' and put some spirit back in the music! And how you know so much 'bout what they call me if you ain't buyin' my records? Huh? You'se a hit dog, Sista Thomas and you doin' a heap uh hollerin'."

I tried hard not to laugh as I made my way back to the back of the church. I fought to get through the crowd, but before I could get there, Christine musta stepped in too close to Brenda to argue back 'cause Brenda laid her out cold. The church was in an uproar. Brenda barred her teeth and said, "I hope to God that knocked some rhythm into you!" She turned on her heels and walked out the door to her car. The deaconess board fanned Christine and dabbed her face with water. Her right eye was already swelling. Brotha Jones and Deacon Thomas tried hard to hold in their laughter in the Amen corner. I looked around for Brenda. She was nowhere in sight.

I tried to get in touch with Brenda and Lucy all that afternoon. They didn't answer the phone or the front door. Brenda didn't show up to Bible class on Wednesday night and I was gettin' worried. During that week, I thought about her different than the one before. I wondered if maybe after she blacked Christine's eye did she run back off to St. Louis. But like nobody expected she would or should, Brenda stepped up in the church proud the next Sunday wearing orange. Instead of stopping at her regular seat on the third pew, she kept walkin' up to the front of the church. She marched right past me up to the choir stand. She stood next to Sista Corrine who smiled at her warmly. Deacon Patterson stopped devotion and the whole church looked at Brenda. Like she didn't even know they was lookin', she kept facing the congregation. After she didn't move, everybody looked at me. I swallowed hard. I knew what they wanted me to do. I nodded to them and stepped in close to Brenda.

"Sista Carson," I whispered to her, "now you know this ain't right. The choir is sposed to agree and vote on you comin' back. As I recall, they ain't yet did that. As pastor of this church, I'm gon' have to ask you to take yo' seat so we can go on wit' the service."

Brenda looked hurt and I felt bad right away. But she did not argue. She stood still, gathered herself, nodded to me and said, "I understand, Pastuh." The looked to her left, squeezed Sista Corrine's hand and stepped down. As quietly as she came in, she left the church. The Holy Spirit didn't show his face in the church too much that Sunday. The pews were filled with talk of how people couldn't believe Brenda had the audacity to do what she did. Christine sat in the soprano section in the choir saying "Amen" and singing louder and more off key than I could ever remember her being before. The crowd lingered longer than they had in all my years as pastor at the church. They dwindled at about four that evening.

I sat to talk with God for a minute. "Jesus, why didn't I let that child sing her song? Who died and gave the hypocrites control of the church, Lord?" Though I am a man of God, I truly understood what Brenda meant when she said that she and Lucy were angry about not getting no answer. I was wondering why The Father didn't answer me this time, too. We normally had such a good line of communication. It seemed as though the Lord gave me the cold shoulder throughout the rest of the week. I started to wonder when He would make His presence known again. I knew things had to be put right for that to happen.

I got in my car and headed over to Lucy and Brenda's house. I figured I might talk to somebody this time since I saw Lucy on the porch when I pulled up. She didn't look as happy to see me as she did the first time but she greeted me anyway.

"Hello, Pastuh Steel. How are you this fine ev'nin'?"

"I'm blessed, Chile. I missed you and your sista at church today. Ain't seen y'all in quite a while."

"Well, we all decided to go to Jasper's church today, Pastuh. No harm done when you still in the Lord, right?"

"You sho' right about that, Baby. You sho' right about that."

I think Lucy knew that I didn't really come to talk to her. She knew who I wanted to talk to and what I wanted to talk about too. So I dropped the act.

"Lucy, is Brenda in this ev'nin? I feel mighty bad about what happened at the church the other Sunday and I might need to set some things right."

"Well, to tell you the truth, Pastuh Steel, I don't think my lil' sister is much for company today. She ain't really said much to nobody lately. But I'll be sho' to tell her you stopped by and ask her to call you soon as she feeling better."

Now I ain't never claimed to be a real smart man. Then again, I never did take it upon myself to be no dumb one neither. I knew what Lucy was tryin' to say was that Brenda wasn't much in the mood for *my* company. But rather than sayin' somethin' and makin' myself feel even worse, I just gave Lucy a nod and a half-hearted smile and was on my way. I drove home that day wondering if I had clipped the wings off of one of God's most precious doves. And a man in that position just don't feel good.

****

It was Mother's Day. Everybody pulled out the biggest hats they could find and pulled out they best smiles right along with them. If I didn't know no better, I would have said that people actually came in the name of Jesus rather than in the name of the designer suits they wore. The devotional part of the service went well. Just as the choir got up to sing, the church doors busted open. Brenda came through wearing a white suit and hat and a stern look on her face. She looked like an angel. And even in the midst of all the bright colors, she still stood out. She approached the front of the church and stood in the center. People began getting to their feet at once. Brenda held up a hand.

"Hold on, Church. This won't take long."

There must have been something either in her words or her tone that frightened them because all of them sat down, shut up and listened. Brenda cleared her throat.

"Now today is Mother's Day," she began, "As many of you may remember, my mother was taken from me at an early age. After that tragedy, me and my sista was sent to live with my Aunt Freda in St. Louis. Now St. Louis is a ways away from Georgia, but news travels fast. I know y'all know 'bout me singin' in the jukes and y'all done seen them lil' outfits I had on on them posters. But I'm here to tell y'all some stuff y'all don't know." I could see her tearing up. "When me and my sista was too young to even be thankin' 'bout womanly thangs, we met sin. We met more than sin. We met *Chicago* Sin. Chicago Sin was my aunt's old man and he had a real knack for business. Well, one day his knack went away and the nightclub him and Aunt Freda was usin' to live off looked like it was gon' get closed down. So, instead of just keeping his business in the juke joint, he decided he needed somethin' else. So, Sin sold me and Lucy to different mens every night. We was told to keep quiet or my sangin' career at The Sack was over. At night we cried and we hurt, but we never told Aunt Freda. She went to her grave loving that man and not even knowin' nothing was wrong. Now me and Piggy didn't stay mad wit' Sin. In them days, folks did what they had to. And mad ain't a wagon you wanna stay hitched up to for too long no how" Brenda swallowed hard. "Me and Lucy lived wit' that til' de Lord saw fit to call Sin home when I was 20. It wasn't no man what give me the name Candy Sweet. Aunt Freda give it to me. She started callin' me Candy 'cause she said I was sweet but she said I was sweeter when I was sangin' so she needed to add a lil' mo' sweet on top. And I

heard a few of y'all whisperin' and wonderin' why I ain't got no husband or no chil'ren," with a tear in her eye, Brenda went on, "Truth is, I want 'em. But I reckon what I went through was too much for my body to bear 'em. And what man wanna be wit' a woman what can't give him no babies?" She looked at the floor for a minute, then smiled at the congregation. "But one thang I got from my mama though was a strong heart," she said, "She give it to me and my sista. So, after all that mess in St. Louis, I decide I'mma come home and see my family so I can get me a lil' mo' strength. But, when I came back, my family turned they back on me. Now, Sista Thomas," she said turning to a black-eyed Christine, "I done apologized to God for what I done to ya'. I only pray even mo' that he forgive me. But we was fussin' 'cause you didn't wanna let me sang." She smirked and held her head high. "But the God I serve 'low his chil'ren to make a testimony every chance they get. I know that I couldn't say the Lord had his way wit' me if I ain't take dis one. Now, I'm sorry for puttin' my hands on ya'. But I ain't sorry a bit for the lessons it mighta taught ya'. Pastuh Steel," she said looking at me wit' Emma's eyes, "you preached that sermon 'bout the prodigal son. But now I gotta ask what the prodigal son is s'posed to do when his father and his family don't welcome him home." She shook her head. "Now, I don't expect you to answer," she said holding up a hand. "Me and the Lord just gotta go out in the world and find out for ourselves. I came back here thinkin' I was gon' find my family. But it's cold. Ain't nobody arms around me to block the wind out. But I don't blame yuh. We speak from what we see and sometimes it's too late fo' we see that good Christians ought not ta' act thataway. I
'member when I was baptized, I thanked you for showin' me where God was. But, I reckon I gotta thank the church fuh showin' me that He don't live here no mo'. I thank y'all for what ya' done for me when me and Lucy was lil' and I pray each and every day that all y'all is blessed."

The church was silent. If you ain't know no better, you woulda thought we was waiting on a funeral. With a smile on her face and tears in her eyes, Brenda nodded to the congregation. With her rope of hair swinging behind her and her story on everybody's hearts, Lil' Brenda Marie Carson walked out the doors of New Canaan Baptist Church into the gleaming Sunday sun.

TK

MISS USED AND ABUSED

Dear Love,

 I hear you when you say you love me. But I'm not sure we have really met. I mean, I know we shook hands and exchanged pleasantries and phone numbers. I know that it's been a year and that you are here with me now. I know you know the name everyone calls me. But I'm not sure you know me by my other name. So, let's start again. Hello. My name is Miss Used And Abused. I am pleased to meet you, but I am terrified at the same time. There is nothing about your appearance or demeanor that scares me. Please know that it's all on me. I know I have told you about my past. But while I was telling you, I hid my scars under the sleeves of a soul sweater that I use so that no one forces me to explain. But the temperature in the room is comfortable now and I want to take this thing off. Because I know you're going to ask me about my marks, I would rather beat you to the punch. The days I seem to wince and back away from you, I am not fearing that you will strike a blow. It is because these bright bruises, crimson cuts, sore scrapes and noticeable knots from ones who came before you have not yet healed. There are parts of me that I am not willing to show you because I am left maimed and somewhat emotionally disfigured by the things they have done. I have not yet regained use of all my feelings and I have been much too embarrassed to show you my handicap. I never wanted to let you guide me around corners when I couldn't see because I was afraid you would realize I'm not as strong as you thought I was. I didn't want to sit still and let you nurse me back to health because I was sure you could never truly love someone so broken. I refused all the pain medication you tried to administer because I didn't want to end up getting too comfortable and falling too deeply in love. This would not allow me to use the defense mechanisms that I always tend to have at the ready. The title of Miss Used And Abused is not one that I have always had. You see, like every little girl, I was once innocent. It wasn't until I met the ones who spoke the words "I love you" prematurely that the appellation became mine. Once they misused and abused me and stole my innocence, there was no other name I could be called. My cuts and bruises still sting sometimes, which may explain my behavior. It's not that I want you to leave. It's just that the things you make me feel are new and exciting and I don't yet have the courage to just let go. Don't get me wrong though. I do want that courage and it is for that reason I have come to formally introduce myself to you. The name is no longer a badge of experience that I am able to wear and come out victorious in any situation. It has instead become a crazed predator that slices me from nose to navel and parades me around in derision. I come to you, skin to the wind, because I want to shed this awful name. Rather than playing the Relationship Rumpelstiltskin and making you guess all the stamps I have on me that make me act this way, I am laying it all on the line. I'm telling you I am Miss Used And Abused in hopes that you have a name more befitting and that you will be patient enough to allow me to live up to it. I am hoping that despite who I have become, you have faith in all I can be. I pray, My Love, that this is not the end.

Sincerely,

Miss Used And Abused (**TK**)

MORNING ROUTINE

I love the way your coffee lingers on your lips.
It waits for me to have a taste
Before it fades away completely.
I am so alive and revived but I can't
Tell if it's from the caffeine or from you.
What about the way the water engulfs you
In the shower but
Takes hold of everything in me at the same time?
It's like an invitation to slide down
Parts of you the streams could never reach.
The way your clothes lay on you-
Shirt over shoulders,
Pants over pelvis,
Shoes over soles-
Makes me take in each part of you as though
It's the first time every time.
I'm amused by your goodbye kiss.
You offer the pleasant peck while
Knowing I will pull you in for much more.
It saddens me when you leave
And it pains me to go my way.
But I harbor wild excitement as I
Ponder all I will do
When I see you again.

TK

When starting new friendships/relationship, are there parts of you that you prefer to keep concealed? Is there a door within you that you prefer remains closed? If so, why?

___
___
___
___
___
___
___
___
___
___
___
___
___
___

THE DOORS

Inside each of us exists a tiny asylum. It's that little bit of crazy that scares us all but fascinates us at the same time. Just as we are our own worst critics, we are not merciful enough to ourselves to make our madhouses state of the art facilities with the best treatment. Instead, we run old chambers of torture with tools and methods as barbaric as our illnesses. We fill them not with rehabilitation but with projections of guilt and perpetuations of punishment. In each of our dirty padded rooms, we lock away pieces of ourselves that only long to be understood. We lock up all we are.

The Lover. We lock The Lover away because we fear that it has enough power to spill over into every part of us. Once so warm, rosy-cheeked and full of life, it now possesses a pallor that makes it unrecognizable. It refuses to be fed and instead lives on the hope of nourishing itself. We lock it away because we are ashamed and grow tired of it allowing itself to be misused. It throws itself upon the floor and screams in vain for the one it wants most. We close the door.

Photo by Michellene Fryson

The Dreamer. We lock The Dreamer away because it reminds us of our own failures. It no longer has the bright eyes and a wild heart we give life to as we sleep. It is gaunt and starved since we have offered up to the foolish Lover its rightful sustenance. We lock it away because we no longer want to fancy ourselves the modern day Sisyphus constantly rolling the lies we have told ourselves up our hill of false promises only to have them roll back down. It pounds upon the wall and screams until its lungs bleed. We close the door.

The Child. We lock The Child away because our own innocence make us feel weak and paltry. Because The Dreamer was its best friend and it, too, is locked away, The Child remains hopeless. In its naivety, it hears the screams around it and still believes in sunshine. It sings its nagging nursery rhymes in hopes of garnering sympathy. We lock it away because it is a reminder of the precious parts of us that will wither and die in spite of us. It sits in the center of the floor rocking and playing with its broken toys without an inkling that it will be forgotten forever. We close the door.

The Whore. We lock The Whore away because it was that thing that we were told never to be. It finds the song of The Child comical because it isn't filled with promises of pleasure or the grunts and moans of passion. The Whore always knew the secrets to never being alone that the pathetic juvenile never could. We lock it away because it is both the center of our shame and the seat of our disgrace. It gyrates against the wall and beckons for a mate that will never come. We close the door.

The Fool. We lock The Fool away because it forces us to find the humor in the things that hurt us most. It is deceptive and makes the punches we take to our guts feel like the incessantly ticklish growth of laughter from our core. It takes the anguish that The Lover invites, the joy The Dreamer believes in, the pain The Child is blind to and the momentary pleasure The Whore nourishes and turns them into the greatest jokes ever told. We lock it away because we fear that if we find the joy, the world will believe we have no hearts or souls. Daftly it somersaults about the room laughing wildly and requesting audience. We close the door.

We never see fit to scrub the walls or sterilize the tools we use to draw out the so-called demons inside of us. We fill our days with pointless rounds of electroshock therapy and prayers for comfort within straitjackets in hopes that we can drive out our own true nature. We convince ourselves of archaic cures and just buy our time until they begin to take hold. We know better but we use these walls as our cloaks. We have no desire to really know ourselves.

We close the door.

TK

THE SHOULDERS I STAND ON

I try to block y'all out sometimes. But you're just too strong. That is really why I love you. On those days that I don't want to get out of bed and would rather just lie there and let the world go on without me, you start speaking so loudly that I don't get a moment's rest. "Get up, Girl," you say, "That's not the way we raised you. You're too much of a warrior to play victim." I drag myself out of bed and stare at myself in the mirror. When I hate the nose on my face and the gray hairs I was born with, when I feel like my thick hips are just weights holding me down, you say "Those are your gifts. Embrace them. Use them wisely." There really are times when I think it would be much easier to JUST be a pretty face. To that, you say "You know what lasts longer than beauty? Being smart." When I think I just want to turn back and pull the covers over my head again, you say "Be passionate and move forward with gusto every single hour of every single day until you reach your goal." I stare hard at my hiding place and contemplate settling back in. But you remind me that there is no peace there either. "Don't stop dreaming just because you had a nightmare," you say. When I join in on conversations and feel like an outsider because I can't identify with a good deal of what is said, you say "You're different. I am too. And that ain't bad. We are limited editions." When I want to shy away from voicing my opinion or replace it with something more socially acceptable, you say "There ain't no substitute for the truth. Either it is or it isn't. See, the truth, it needs no proof. Either it is or it isn't." When I drop my head and almost lose my crown, you say "Think like a queen. A queen is not afraid to fail. Failure is another steppingstone to greatness." When I want to do things halfway, you say "Don't settle for average. Bring your best to the moment." I have felt defeated. But your voice booms saying "The moment anyone tries to demean or degrade you in anyway, you have to know how great you are." I feel weak sometimes. But you say "I love you. YOU keep me strong." I want to carry my baggage sometimes. But instead of judging me, you wipe my tears and wrap an arm around me saying "Girl, I know sometimes it's hard and we can't let go…Pack light". And when the world gets extra bitter, with your hands on your hips, you add "Honey, YOU so sweet. Suga got a long way to catch you."

Thank you, Mama. Thank you, Grandma. Thank you, Aunt El. Thank you, Aunt Tan. Thank you, Gabrielle Union. Thank you, Ava DuVernay. Thank you, Jill Scott. Thank you, Jallisa. Thank you, Ladara. Thank you, India Arie. Thank you, Oprah. Thank you, Angela Bassett. Thank you Cicely Tyson. Thank you, Monika. Thank you, Erykah Badu. I thank you all. And I pray you go on speaking forever.

TK

WHO NEEDS A SONG?

I don't need a song to tell me I'm in love with you.
I don't need anyone to rhyme maybes with baby
Or give me a sweet falsetto to know that you're everything to me.
Yeah, a nice little tune to slow dance to is nice
But it's not required.
It doesn't take two verses or 16 bars for me to fall for you,
I do that every time I breathe anyway.
My heart doesn't beat the same anymore.
Now it whispers your name.
It's new.
It's improved.
I mean, I appreciate a good melody as much
As the next girl.
But until they can all sing in the key of you,
They are unacceptable.
Yeah, maybes and baby,
Love and above,
Together forever through any weather—
They're all cool.
But they're nothing I haven't heard before.
I'd rather take off my headphones
And press my ear to your soul instead.

TK

I'm trynna be your ampersand.
I wanna be that thing that completes
The puzzle of you **&** I.
I wanna be the one that makes love
Make sense when it stands next to happiness.
I don't wanna be a comma or colon for you
Because I plan to love you without pause.
And I would never play period
Because I plan to continuously adore you
With no stops.
Sometimes, I ponder being a exclamation point
But that's just so everybody would hear me
When I shout about you.
Question mark is not my goal
Since I have never been more sure about anyone.
You wouldn't need me as a semicolon
Because I plan to do more than just connect us.
I plan to merge our souls.
I would **NEVER** be an apostrophe.
I don't own you, but I want to **BECOME** you.
I want to be seen in the way you
Walk
Talk
Exist.
Your ampersand is what I choose because
When trials meet tribulations,
When joy meets pain,
When ups meet downs
And the smoke clears,
I want to be all you see.
So I'm trynna be your ampersand.
Let me be the one that puts you together.

TK

MY G-BIRD

There are wrinkles in the corners of her eyes. But that's only because over the years, she has seen so many lessons that caused them to open wider. It's pretty similar to the way your new wallet starts to crease the more it is opened. She wears them proudly because it took her a long time to earn them. She had to carry an entirely smooth face for a while since she hadn't quite learned enough. And those gray strands in her hair are no bother. The old wives tale says gray hair is a sign of experience and wisdom. God must have known that she would be a wise one. After all He saw fit to give her a few strands at birth so that everyone would see that she "has been here before". Those slightly crooked fingers of hers, though painful at times, are beautiful almond badges of honor. She has used them to fight a number of battles in the name of her family over the years. From cooking to cleaning to sewing to knitting and jewelry-making, they have helped her to keep food on the table and peace in the home.

It hurts when she walks but she does it anyway. There is a certain joy to being able to do the things you were told you could never do again. As she looks back on 1975, she takes another step. Each one tells that big broken oak tree that laid upon her 'You pinned me. But you didn't win me'. She moves about her old house every day relishing in the memories within the walls. Looking at the faces in the frames on the walls, she is always amazed at how even the most reserved of her children and grandchildren inherited that storytelling smile of hers. They are greater than anything she could have ever created with a knitting needle. She can't move the way she used to and she lays no claim to being educated. She has never seen a million dollars but she is the richest woman in the world.

As she settles down in her rocking chair, she closes her eyes and smiles. "Lord, this life ain't been easy. But I just thank you that I am still here livin' it."

TK

MY MAMA

Let me just be real with y'all. There are some days I feel like when the Great Daughter Draft Pick took place a few decades ago, my mother did not go home with a first-round pick. But the fact that that is **MY** assessment of myself and has never been hers is the main reason why I adore her. I attempted to put my ideas about my mother into poetry (which I have done on a few occasions) but it just didn't work as well for me when it came to telling the world who she is. I mean, I could have found some grand Shakespearean way to say "My mama is a badass", but I just decided to make it plain. Even though I had no way of knowing her when she was little, I think my mama was pretty amazing in her youth. Whether she was beating up a boy who picked on her in the neighborhood (see "broke his collar bone") or coping with the pain of losing a child and being a wife at the same time right after having to decide what to do with her life after high school, the lady was already conquering. Oh and I still maintain that NOBODY rocked a pair of white majorette shorts and a red afro better. Seriously Millennials, be seated because you have yet to meet the master. The oldest of all of her siblings, my mother is the best example of both sibling and maternal love I have ever seen. Even though they don't always agree, I am in awe of the way my aunts and uncles look to her for strength and support. She and G-Bird shared the task of mothering and even to this day, they all seem to breathe easier just knowing the both of them are near.

    I did say that I was rough around the edges, right? I like to think that a lot of it comes from the fact that I am like Mama was when she was younger. When she told me about climbing trees, playing softball and sneaking into the blackberry patches when she knew better, it only inspired me. I know that these days, everyone calls their daughters princesses. I have no problem with that but that was not how my mother did things. Instead of dressing me in pink (which she did try and still tries every now and then) and telling me stories about a prince coming to rescue me, she reiterated the ways in which I would earn my crown and ways I could rescue myself. When I would get good grades in school and when I wrote my first poem in kindergarten, she was my biggest cheerleader. In anything she did, I was always her little sidekick. When she cooked, I was right next to her messing up until I learned to do it right. When she did her makeup, I was there next to her making myself look like the victim of a tragic crayon explosion. I have fond memories of sitting on the floor between her knees while she blessed my pigtails with Blue Magic and Royal Crown. Conversely, I remember her wrath when I decided I would cut off one of those pigtails and half my bangs. When I graduated kindergarten, I remember running into her arms after being just as exciting as the diploma I crushed between us. I watched her raise the coolest man on the planet (shouts out to my big brother Brandon) and give love a second chance and nail it perfectly after it was so unkind to her initially. Mama is still that same nurturing soul these days. She is so giving of herself, her time and resources. Even when she is hurt and used, her first reaction is to love. I knew that whether my first book or any I would ever write was a success or a huge flop, she would love me and still call me her favorite author. Even though I feel like I fall short, to her, I am exquisite. She makes the rest of the world feel like they are lacking because they didn't get me in that Great Daughter Draft Pick. I will admit that I gloat when it comes to her too. She's my mama, My Shuga. And can't nobody tell me she ain't fly.

TK

DEAR WHITE BEST FRIEND,

I'm a second-class citizen. I don't see myself that way and I know that's not how you see me. But that is the way America sees me and my unborn children. You see, they will be born with a cross to bear. And until they get here, the splinters of said cross will be content to draw their blood from me instead. The only crime that ever had to be committed was to show up with black skin. Our heartbreak is not what matters in any court of law. Our tears are only meant to water seeds of hatred. We all live not with thoughts of what we will be when we grow up, but what we want to TRY to be IF we grow up. Long gone are the days of drinking from separate fountains but we cannot pretend our thirsts are quenched when the streets run red with our blood. They might as well show me my sonogram and send me on my way with a set of baby booties with shackles attached because we are all expected to be in them from birth.

I love you every day and every minute you are my sister. But there are times we have been on the run from reality. Hand in hand we flee through the woods and wade through muddy rivers. But the dogs aren't trained to smell you. We stand in forests facing our fates, but the nooses are not made for your neck. We move in the night with only a lantern to see, but you don't need to run to find your freedom.

When I shut down, know that you are not the source of my avoidance. Also know that when we discuss headlines, not only do I have to rationalize, but I have to fear for my brothers and my offspring. My babies are robbed of breath before knowing the joy. Know that I am trying to process the conversation I had with one of my beautiful dark skinned sisters who told me she would only date and marry a white man so that her children can be lighter and have an easier life than she did. Know that I am trying to process the fact that someone who isn't Black can garner a million laughs from pretending to be us, but when the curtain closes, they get to walk down the street and go home safely. Know that I am mad as hell, but I am doing my best to be civil and not display that Angry Black People Syndrome they say we are all born with. Know that I know your eyes are not the only ones on me and that not all lips are speaking of me favorably. Know that I am trying to hold it all together. Know that I am doing the best that I can.

Sincerely,
TK

BRAELYNN

I plan to give you the world every time I see you.
But every time, I fall short.
I have lived a few decades.
You have yet to see one
But you have given me so much already.
From the first time you opened your eyes
And smiled at me, I felt welcome.
From the way you look at your father and open
Rooms in his heart that I never knew existed,
To the first time your pudgy hands
Smoothed my hair back and said I was beautiful
To the smile you gave even though you
Couldn't understand why that made me cry
To the way you still snuggle up next to me
Even though you're getting older
To the way you always trust me to save the world
Even though some days I am too weak to save myself—
When you say you love me,
Your voice is like wind chimes,
I close my eyes and listen.
And no matter who calls me "Ti-Ti",
No one says it the way you do.
I am inspired as I watch you love life
Even though some of the things you are faced with
Are far beyond your years.
I am honored that you are a part of me.
I haven't been able to give you the world
The way I have always planned.
But I promise to keep trying
For as long as I am allowed.

TK

LYING ON YOUR FACE

You are his page.
The story he writes on you is a long one.
I appreciate the way he takes care to make it match the one
That comes out of your mouth.
You pantomime his "It won't happen again" perfectly.
And you listen intently as he convinces you that it was your fault.
He feeds you "I only do it because I love you" by the spoonful.
Frankly, I am impressed you can eat it all through swollen lips.
His fist splashes "Why did you make me do it?" across your cheeks.
He smears "Bitch, if you leave me, I'll find you" around your eyes.
For good measure, he dabs a bit of "Please don't leave me. I'll get help"
On your forehead.
He adds pops of "No one else will ever love you"
And shades of "All of this is your fault".
He tops it all off with "I own you" and "Get cleaned up.
We're going out tonight".
I know you cry.
I know it's a story of lies you read through the blur of tears.
But I can only hope you'll tear out those pages someday
And do some writing of your own.

TK

If you or anyone you know needs help, please call the National Domestic Abuse Hotline at 1-800-799-7233. Find additional resources at www.thehotline.org.

I HAD A VISITOR

Sadness came to see me today.

I invited her to sit next to me.

I asked her about her travels and how she made it from my ancestors to me so quickly.

She explained that the side door usually is easy for her to get into.

She has a cousin named Joy but she doesn't get in as easily.

Joy, being so light and agile, has to knock first.

And because she is too busy enjoying being herself,

She never bothers to memorize passwords or secret handshakes to get through.

She can rarely charm her way past the porch so she moves on down the road.

But Sadness— so heavy and dark, so layered in the soot of herself—

Always seems right at home with us.

She basically just walks right in.

She walks by and brushes up against us.

But my ancestors and I—heavy, dark people, so covered in the soot of ourselves—

Don't always notice.

She clings to our skin and the spirits of our past so often

We begin to think she belongs there.

No one ever really asks who she belongs to.

They just assume she has always been ours.

When she gets a little tired from her housework, she'll sit on the porch

Or take a little stroll in the yard but she doesn't go far.

While she takes a break, she lets Contentment take over.

Joy took off down the road a long time ago but Contentment looks enough

Like her to be a nice replacement.

I am always in awe of the pleasantries the two of them exchange as they trade posts.

I sat and talked with Sadness today because I wanted to understand her better.

She told me her history and all of her hopes and dreams.

She told me how she longed to be something different.

She held my hands in hers and reminisced on all the lessons we had learned together.

She is comfortable here but we both want better for me.

We both want to prepare a permanent place for Joy.

Sadness wants to become a less frequent visitor.

She wants to separate herself from me,

Leaving only her lessons behind.

TK

A GROOVE FOR MIDNIGHT

Can you help me?
I wanna tell you about Love,
But I've never seen it.
Yes Love, we are in love
But I couldn't see us as we were falling.
      I never saw Love wrap its arms around my waist,
      Woo me, screw me, but make me chaste.
      I know it happened.
      I just never saw it.
Never saw it turn my face toward the sun
Create light when the day is done,
Make sense of two becoming one,
I never saw it…
But I know it happened.
      Never saw it give unto me the sweetest taboo,
      Sex me but give me virgin's value,
      Turn a gray sky five new shades of blue.
      I never saw it….
But here I am.
I've not seen, but felt the joy within,
The joy of touching paper to pen,
The pride of committing the sweetest sin…
But I can't write about what I haven't seen.
      I've never seen, but I have felt,
      The thrill of having your body melt,
      Too out of breath to sing, but wanting to belt.
      Hmmm…..Maybe I can write about the feeling.
The feeling of your lips pressing to mine,
The violation I feel when your body comes to mind
The intense sting of wanting to be entwined
Maybe…..
I'll write about you.
      Your touch--soft and warm like melting butter,
      Your speech, be it strong, or low, loving mutter.
      The way you make me st-st-stutter
      Oh yeah……
I'll write about you.
The long looks you take into my eyes,
The way submission is a blessing in disguise,
How I am dumbfounded, but simultaneously wise
Don't get me started talking about you.
      How you run a finger down the small of my back
      How my chemistry and yours reacts
      How I'm still not sure just how I should act
      When I'm around you.

How you hold me close and oh so safely,
Erase all "no", "never" and "maybe",
How I just can't sit still here lately.
Damn.
Now I know that love is you.

> You are the success of my endeavor.
> Just by writing about us together,
> I've written all about love and I will never…
> Know love without having you.

TK

A LESSON IN LILIES

My lilies died to teach me a lesson. I know that now I was supposed to learn quite a few. The first was that no matter how much I love something or how beautiful I think it is, sometimes it's just not meant to last. I may scramble to nourish it, solicit opinions, do research and run myself ragged trying to keep it alive. But if it isn't what's meant to grow, all of my effort is for naught. When my lilies were alive, I knew they were average, every day 7.4" Flare Calla Lilies. But there was something about my lilies that just made them special. They were brighter and more beautiful than any I had ever seen. They grew in the same soil as the ones that had been next to them at the store and they were of the same exact genus. But I still felt like mine were better. It's like that sometimes. Sometimes all it takes is for something to be *yours* for it to be the very best. Those times when my lilies would wither when they had seen too much sun, but still showed a little bit of life, showed me that even though circumstances changed, they would eventually come back to me. That let me know that sometimes what sounds like "no" is simply "not right now". Even after they died, and I mean REALLY died, the brown of their hardened petals was still beautiful. The way they still reached out and somehow froze themselves in a pose that showed no sign of surrender was majestic to me. Though harder than they once were, the leaves around the lilies still curved and curled flirtatiously as if to say "Oh, that's not all". Like a starlet on her deathbed, the body is not as lively as before but the beauty lives on. I believe my lilies will be back. And if they never return, I am grateful for the lessons they have left behind.

TK

IN HIS HAIR

There's poetry in his hair.
At first, I thought I was losing my mind.
But it's real.
His kinks and coils dance around one another to
Emphasize his points.
The rhyme scheme is strict and because he is
Poignant without pause, he wastes no time with putting in parts.
His edges are tapered and neat to be sure
I never fall off.
In serious situations, it is closely cropped-
You know, nice and low with a sea of deep waves I can vibe to.
When he really wants me to feel his presence, he grows it a little higher
To make sure I take notice.
He lets me run my fingers through his pentameter
To be sure we connect.
He keeps me listening.
He keeps me guessing.
He keeps me indefinitely.

TK

ACCEPTANCE

Good morning, Natural Hair. You and I have made amends for all of my ignorance to what those chemicals did to you. I finally wised up and gave you the chance to be what you have been all along. And just like I don't judge the ones who still dance with chemicals, no one can judge me for wearing you straight instead of in a 'fro. We can boast about the fact that we left the "creamy crack" alone years ago. We flow a little more when the wind blows. I love you.

How are you, Brown Eyes? I don't care at all anymore that your lashes are short. That just means we are not blinded by certain things. You don't have to be hazel to mesmerize and the messages you send can weaken knees and send hearts aflutter. Not large, not small- you don't give away many secrets. I am amazed at the things you've seen. I love you.

Well hello, Round Nose! There has always been something special about you. You are the perfect combination of weird and just right that keeps people intrigued. But instead of being an object of confusion, you are more of a beacon of interest. You're lucky because I have always loved you.

Greetings, Full Lips. I really don't look at you the same as I used to. You used to be blemishes to me, the things that made my face not quite right. Now you are jewels to me instead. I see you as resting places for the poetry I have been blessed with. You are those parts of me where I can let the words drip down slowly before I give anyone else a chance to digest them. You are magnifiers of my lore. I love you.

Shine in, Smile. You aren't a perfect white, but you are so perfect when you're honest. Sometimes you alone are responsible for bringing light to my face. The subtle messages you and my eyes send back and forth to each other happen so fast but you translate into the universal language of happiness. I miss you when you're not there, so I promise to always find reasons for you to come back. I never realized it before. But I love you.

Salutations, Torso. You are a community and I embrace all who live within you. Breasts, I once thought you too small and thought you stayed the way you were to spite me. Little did I know you knew what the rest of me was to become and always stayed proportioned. Belly, you have changed much over the years. And though your current size is not my favorite, I can count on you to be the faithful sign of whether or not I am treating myself well. Belly Button, you don't make yourself known, but thanks to the war wound you don, you cannot be ignored. You're probably not considered pretty, but you have a story to tell. You trade lines of it with Breasts and Belly. And I love you all.

Hi, Hips and Thighs (or My Hams and Yams as I affectionately call you)! I have always loved the way it feels when you move to my favorite song. But it took me a while to come to terms with the way you look. You have always been much bigger than what I have seen in any magazine and you certainly looked nothing like the mannequins I saw in the stores. That led me to believe there was something wrong with you. Then I noticed that when those models and mannequins were dressed, they couldn't draw the lines or make the curves you do. Sure you have a couple of dents and lumps here and there. But after feeling the way you sway and realizing you are art, none of that matters. All that matters is that I love you.

How are you Knees? You are a bit scarred from that eleventh birthday when we decided to be Evil Knievel. When it all went down, I didn't shed any tears. Instead, I just thought about what cool war wounds I would have after my little stunt. I didn't know that in later days that when it came to shorts and skirts, I would become embarrassed and want to hide you instead of boasting about my guts. Maybe it was just a case of growth because now I look at you and say "I was young. That was dumb. But I love you".

We meet again, Legs. I've told you about the growth of my appreciation for you. But it seems other people are occasionally feeling the same. Once upon a time, I considered you stubbly little annoyances but now I am realizing all the places you can take me. I'm glad to get you dancing again. I know how much you missed it. And Honeys, we've got reasons! You never deserved any of the abuse I gave you. I'm sorry and I love you.

Looking good, Fingers and Toes! It's amazing how I have taken you for granted over the years. But I am noticing you more now. Toes, I never appreciated the flair you bring my stilettos. You sure do make a peep toe pop! And fingers, you bring interest whether it's with a new nail color, a gesture or a strong standing middle digit when someone gets out of line. I never realized how much you all did before. But I do now and I love you.

Hey, Booty! I used to get upset when you became the topic of conversation. But nowadays, I don't mind mentioning you myself. At one point very early in life, you were the subject of ridicule. Now you are a coveted characteristic and the task at hand in many an operating room across the globe. You jiggle when I walk sometimes. But that just adds a little more music to my stride. I love you.

Hello, TK. I have seen you every day all of my life. But it has only been until recently that we've REALLY met. I have put you through so much. But I am hoping you can forgive me and enjoy every moment of life with me. I love you and I accept you.

TK

BUBBA

You deserve a cape. For the whole of my life, you have been a hero. Again and again, you have been faced with new situations and you have shined through them all. I'm guilty of always looking at you as the golden child—the one everyone loves and the one who never had to go far to find a friend. But I didn't always listen to your heart the way I should have. I missed out on a lot of great stories that way. I heard from a distance the way it broke in the hands of a woman who had no clue how to care for it. I have seen that same heart race when when those little brown eyes that you have seen grow wiser over the years look up at you and that tiny voice says "I love you, Daddy". I have seen that heart be confused when it wanted to be sure it was loving correctly. I have seen that heart grow wild with the excitement of new love. Your heart is strong but it has hurt. It has never deserved to. I love to see your heart do that thing where it smiles and runs free. I love to see it hope and love and laugh out loud even when no one else can hear the joke. You and your heart deserve all the joy in the world. You're a king, Big Brother. And I will give you a new crown every day, for all eternity.

TK

Photo by Reggie Raphael Wallace

MOMENTS FOR LIFE

I need a bottle of these moments,
A repository of perfection to unleash on those not-so-right times.
That way, I can always have the sun on your face
Just like this.
I can always see slivers of its rays laying gently on your shoulders
As they play coyly about the sheets.
I will always have your aroma surrounding me
Driving me into a sensual stupor.
I will always have your arms skirting around my waist and
Feel your breath on my ear.
I will always hear that faint groggy moan that says nothing intelligible
But explains my entire existence.
I will never have to wonder the reward for opening my eyes.

TK

GOODBYE FOREVER

"Goodbye forever" has never been a phrase
That rolled off my tongue easily.
That was until today.
This morning I woke up and recognized
The beauty of a sunrise.
I saw the flowers continue to grow in spite of everything.
I felt the beat of my own heart and
Moved with the blood as it flowed through me.
I noticed all the things the universe still deemed me worthy of
And got full off of my own energy.
I heard my own voice and achieved
Peace in the moment.
I love you.
But I no longer live you.

TK

Photo by Reggie Raphael Wallace

THIRSTY

I am never thirsty when I drink from you.
Regardless, just the sight of your thoughts brewing makes me want
A fourth cup before I have even had the first.
I follow your ebb and flow and fall into your rhythm.
You wash over me as I sleep and rid me of the
Grime of trying days.
Each morning, I am privileged to dive in again.
I want for nothing.
I am entirely quenched by you.

TK

Photo by TK Long

DRUNK

I could use another shot of you.
Or maybe I need a whole fifth.
I have been drinking you in for a while
But I am still thirsty.
I need more of that buzz,
That precious haze that makes me forget everything.
I need more of that intoxicating tickle that
Makes me laugh without cause.
I want that fear of falling so that
I can have the joy of feeling you catch me.
I never get the nausea so I get
To enjoy all of the pleasantries.
I crave that moment where an inferno grows within me.
I desperately need to wake up on the floor of you.

TK

LIVE TO DREAM (in Memory of the Beautiful Souls of Pulse Orlando)

Sometimes I dream of who you might have been.
I'm sure you did too.
As you went about your day,
You didn't know it was the end for you.
Be it another day at school
Or a night out to laugh and dance
You probably planned to recount it all for me
As soon as you had the chance.
Your heart raced with joy and happiness,
The same as any other day.
Not once did you have an inkling that
Someone would take it all away.
You never had a chance to say goodbye
But I'm sure you never knew you should.
You never said you were sorry
But you knew I knew you would.
You would have called me in the morning
To talk about last night.
By the time you said you loved me,
I would have forgotten all about that fight.
The smile on my face would have made yours
A lot bigger.
I would have pulled you closer to me
Had no one ever pulled the trigger.
I would have wrapped you in my arms.
I would have covered you in love.
But now you lie there all alone
With only a blanket of your blood.
They never bothered to get to know you.
They never asked you your name.
But because they only saw themselves,
Life will never be the same.
They never knew they could have loved you.
They never knew you could be friends.
They never knew you wanted to heal the world
Before it all came to an end.
They never got to know your mother.
They never knew how you made her smile.
They never cared that they would leave a void by

Taking away her child.
They can blame it on religion.
But it's cowardice and unjust fear.
Just being honest,
Those are the real reasons that
You're not here.
The memories and fantasies are all I have left, it seems.
But I wonder what could have possibly been
If you had been left alive to dream.

TK

Photo by Reggie Raphael Wallace

SOMETIMES

Sometimes you feel better than that song
That reminds me of that one time.
Sometimes you remind me of the summer sun on my skin and sitting
Under the tree at G-Bird's house.
Sometimes you remind me of the first time I read Zora and that pounding in my heart
Sparked from knowing
That I had been moved.
Sometimes you remind me of
Light rain upon my face,
Bad conditioning for my hair but
The perfect melody for dancing.
Sometimes you remind me of dorm room sit-downs
So filled with hope and promise for the future.
Sometimes you feel like that time I scraped up my knees, the burning pain
Of knowing I will wear these scars forever.
Sometimes you feel like that after softball sweat
Mixed with dirt and fatigue
With the road to rest growing longer.
Sometimes you remind me of that Lauryn Hill CD—
The one I played until it was scratched—
The sadness of ruined greatness only bested by knowing that at such a late hour,
I have to wait to replace it.
Sometimes you are the soreness of mosquito bites
And the annoyance of them taking days to disappear.
Sometimes you are that feeling of having so much to say but knowing no one speaks your language.
Sometimes you are 4am,
That up spilling heartache on paper
Because I know I can't call you kinda feeling.
Sometimes I can't stand you.
But sometimes you are all that matters.
Sometimes I wish it wasn't so.

TK

EVERYTHING AND NOTHING

He makes me feel everything and nothing at all.
He has become my panicked heartbeat and that
Saturday morning feeling of calm with nothing to do
And nowhere to be.
He is that feeling of being full but at the same time
That growling hunger in the pit of my stomach.
Thanks to him, I have become a glorious glutton.
The more I get, the more I want.
But I want nothing more than more of him.
There are stories in his smile and
Pure poetry in his eyes.
I listen to every line of him and
Wrap myself in his rhymes.
His touch is pure magic
And I am happy to be his lovely assistant.
But I have to stick around if the trick goes wrong.
If the zigs and zags of his saw aren't just right,
I could be cut in half.
But for him, I bleed with gratitude.
He is my peace.
He is my thin air.
He is the heaviness of all the world upon my shoulders.
He is my blank canvas,
My missing link.
He is what brings me to life.

TK

LOCK & KEY

I searched for my keys
But I found your heart instead.
It happened last night as you yelled
That you hated me.
It was right between the reasons you wish
You had never met me and the fact that
You should have listened when "they" told you
I was no good.
In your eyes, I saw the pang of guilt the words
Drizzled across your taste buds.
As your hands shook, I could see how much
They wanted to touch me.
You might have thrown a glass at the wall but I could tell
You wanted nothing more than
To throw yourself into me and apologize
For all you were thinking.
As I cried and insisted you never loved me
My voice shook because I knew you
Loved me best.
The tears formed in my eyes for fear
That you might believe even half of what I said.
Our words met like dragons in mid-air but
Rather than a fiery fight to the finish,
They rested in satisfying submission.
Exhausted from screaming wasted words,
A simple touching of hands gives the
"I'm sorry" and "I didn't mean what
I said" that could have
Saved us from all this madness.
Maybe I couldn't find my keys because
I knew that nowhere else I could have gone
Would have done justice to my presence.
And that has to be how I ended up here-
Legs on legs,
Fingers entwined,
Lips locked,
Tangled up in you.

TK

Photo by Michellene Fryson

HAPPY VALENTINE'S DAY

Kiss my ass, Cupid.
You don't deserve a holiday.
Who was it who told you you were welcome anyway?
      You shoot your little arrows
      And they hit all the wrong places.
      You keep people blind to real love
      Right in front of their faces.
Instead, you send them on a quest.
You make them look for things anew
And overlook the only one who has the heart to stay true.
      You break too many hearts.
      You put real emotions on shelves.
      You make those without sweethearts feel worse about themselves.
Someone should rip off your wings
And pull the curls from your hair.
If someone kicked your naked ass, I can't say that I'd care.
      Wipe that grin off your face.
      You've made today all about facades and money.
      When there is no real love on the "Day of Love",
      What on earth is so damn funny?
      I should break those damn arrows.
      They're useless anyway.
      They tell people they should wait and give Love on just one day.
      Please don't get me wrong.
      It's a day I'm blessed to see.
      But he doesn't have to give the world
      On February 14th to say he loves me.
He can write me a poem on a random day.
He can give me a rose or two.
He can hold me in his arms
And I promise that'll do.
      You hit the girl across the street
      With that big shiny ring.
      You let the almighty dollar rob her of everything.
She doesn't know the joys
Of a quiet night at home.
Without the designer labels he gives her,
She is utterly alone.
      Thank you, Winged Asshole.
      You didn't think before you pulled your trigger.
      Now lovers focus on the small gifts and
      Overlook the bigger.
THEY are the gifts.
They should treasure one another.
Stupid Cupid, you should never have a bigger impact on them
Than they have on each other.

On February 14th.
They should put you in your place.
When you urge them to show love only then,
They should laugh in your fat face.

Those who understand their hearts don't need you.
You can be on your way.
They're smart enough not to just fall for someone
On International Buy Me A Bear Day.

Go away, but not empty-handed.
Since it's love of which you speak,
With love, you can kiss my ass
From cheek to robust cheek.

TK

BOBBY

You were my very best friend at one point. But we will probably never see each other again. As heavy as that may sound, much of our time together, I look back on with gratitude rather than regret. It's because of you, I know how it feels to really be a friend to the one who loves you. Really neither of us knew what we were doing or how to love each other. But once we decided to just let go and BE, we accepted one another wholeheartedly. You always had this way of looking at me that made everyone else in the room disappear. Once they were gone, we would have a full conversation without ever parting our lips. It would usually end in laughter because at heart, we were both some of the goofiest people I knew. But we loved each other and we did so purely.

We didn't meet at the crossroads of our lives but we definitely walked there together arm and arm. We ended up walking in opposite directions and I think we held on to faith that if we walked slowly, we would never lose sight of one another. But there was a storm going on on my part of the road that I couldn't tell you about. It shook up everything in my world and when you would call out to me, I couldn't answer for the dust and debris caught in my throat. I did cry, but my pride and the constant whirl of the wind were strong enough to dry my tears before anyone could see them. I wanted to talk to you but I choked on the words. Some of that might have been my own doing because I wanted to protect the others who were in the storm with me. And even if it meant opening a window so that I could see outside, I had to concentrate on the possibility of what was outside getting in. That overtook me. So, I pushed myself away from the window. I pushed myself farther from you. As a sort of opposition to when I walked in the opposite direction of you at our crossroads, I hoped that as I pushed myself away, I would get out of earshot of your breaking heart. I always hoped that you would just forget about me so that I would never have to tell you just how messed up I was. You deserved better but every time I planned to tell you I didn't love you anymore or that I had found someone else, I was turned off by what lies those were. So I stayed there, swirling in my cloud. Meanwhile, you never even knew that it was raining.

TK

SOMETIMES I AM LOVE

Sometimes I am love.
My spirit tingles and my soul radiates
With the euphoria of simply being.
My senses are finally gifted unto me.
I exist in the way I've always wanted to.
Everything looks brighter.
I see as I've never seen.
The smallest atom of all that I hold dear
Magnifies itself.
I can even hear the breaths the hummingbird takes
During her song and there is music in them too.
Every nerve in me is awake and
Even the slightest touch from the wind thrills me.
I can taste the joy in the smiles of others
And I take long sips of satisfaction.
It's true that I can smell fear, but I never miss
The scent of the flower fields of hope that mask it.
I spread my arms and wave my hands over them,
Making sure the fragrance travels.
I share with the world what it feels like
To float on air and to know that
You are one with everything around you.
I give the awareness of purpose and the
Soul soothing silk of revelation.
Love is never a journey
But a simple appreciation for one's own place in
The now.

TK

IF ONLY

I've been watching you.
The way you stand strong like a statue and pretend you don't know
Everyone is in awe of your majesty.
I love the way you pretend you don't know
That I long to taste the words that lay upon your lips.
I love the way you act as though when each ripple of your body
Thrusts into me,
You don't see my eyes roll back in my head.
It's cute how you try and act as though there is nothing special
About your skin.
Like Crayola ever created a color called Perfection or like any palate
Holds shades to mix for Totality.
I like the way those eyes of yours set the blaze
And let my mind kiss down that face of yours to that smile
Where the fire becomes wild.
I never like to see you leave, but I do so love to watch you
Walk away
As you always leave behind a smile and a stream of purely impure thoughts.
Oh, I know you know I've been watching you.
But if only you knew what I was thinking.......

TK

WHAT IS MUSIC?

Music is as the raging sea-
An endless crashing of waves.

Music is as a first-time hero-
Forever linked to all that it saves.

The rhythms are as massages-
Soothing to every body part.

These rhythms are as vital veins-
Essential to the heart.

The lyrics are as strong bones-
A strong body's only frame.

The lyrics are as mothers-
Calling each child by its full name.

The choruses are as pillows-
Resting places for the head.

These choruses are as lost souls-
Desperately seeking to be led.

Music is as a folktale-
Never secretive and always retold

Music is as salvation-
The best friend of a dying soul.

TK

SLIPPERY SLOPE

I think I must have slipped off your mind again.
It's funny how that happens when you get a little busy.
Or maybe it happens when she comes back around and
Things seem good.
You forget to think of me during those times but
The rest of the time, you remember my name better than your own.
On those late nights and the days she doesn't strike your fancy,
I am all over your brain.
It seems that even your heart beats in syllabic rhythm with my footsteps.
I lay lavishly on your tongue as every word you speak
Is chased by me as though you are some obsessive compulsive drunk
Who just can't stop throwing me back.
I show up in your smile and invade every song you hear on the radio.
When you turn on your TV, I am the star in every role.
I am the model for every painting and sculpture you see and
No revolution of your world happens without me.
I know I pay the price of not coming before her because
When she pokes her head back in, the door closes on me.
Together, you and she ride the same merry-go round you have for years.
It's fun at first.
You giggle and hold hands.
But soon, each spin leaves you nauseous and throwing up
To purge yourself of the soured joy that has run its course.
Clumsily you stumble off the creaky, pointless, God-forsaken ride
And seek comfort.
You look around for me, the one who knows how to soothe that ache
And dab my cool waters on your forehead to bring forth stillness
In your world again.
You look for me to caress your belly until it quivers no more and
Make you feel whole again.
Not once do you give any thought to the sickness I may be feeling
From being a by-stander as you go round and round with her.
Never does it occur to you that I have aches that need soothing
Or that my throbbing head may need a cradle.
You don't care that I compromised myself to stand in line for even a moment
To see if you would ever be ready to love me truthfully.
But you see, I am fine with it all.
I may have slipped off your mind, but you never *slipped* off mine.
Instead, I threw back my shoulders, saw my worth
And PUSHED you off with great pleasure.

TK

JUST ANOTHER SHADE OF PRETTY

Dark-skinned. Tar baby. Blackie. Midnight. They might call you all these things. But I just call you beautiful. I look at the way your eyes and smile shine brightly against that glorious canvas you call skin. It is the same canvas that when you dance and perspire, reminds me of water cascading off chocolate. So it is like the craving and the quenching all in one. In your skin, you carry the breaths of kings and queens who helped to shape this world. I just call you beautiful.

Light-skinned. Redbone. High yella. Lite brite. Sometimes they call you these things. But I just call you beautiful. I look at the way your hair shines, using your skin as a base for its natural highlights. Oh, that skin. It is the same shade as café au lait, the same shade as a walnut. So it kinda goes down smooth but has the potential to be the thing that sticks in your throat and forces you to take notice. You won't be ignored. I just call you beautiful.

You see into each other. You stare at one another and study each curve and crevice, every shade of every scar. You wrap around each other and hug every bit of peace and pain the other has to offer. You celebrate one another. Dark-skinned, Tar baby, Blackie, Midnight and Light-skinned, Redbone, High yella, Lite Brite—You bask in the beauty that is your sisterhood.

TK

TAKE ME OR LEAVE ME

I walk with my head up high
Because the rain yields for me.
It feeds exotic flowers by the field for me.

I speak boldly
Because I know what I'm talking about.
I know there is good sense in everything that comes out.

I sing really loudly
Because I know I'm always in the right key.
Even if I don't feel like being a sparrow, it feels pretty good to me.

I bat my eyelashes
Because I know I have the power to seduce.
Because I know what he likes doesn't mean I'm fast or loose.

I am showing a little leg
Are you afraid he's paying attention?
Or that he notices my conversation and your booty is all that he mentions?

I love sports
And I'm not too girly to play.
That is one reason he and I will never run out of things to say.

I dance when I don't hear music
Because there is freedom when I sway my hips.
Life is a replenishing cup of rhythm best enjoyed at a slow sip.

I am unforgettable
And the world will know me long after I'm gone.
That's how it is, so take me or leave me alone.

TK

AWAKE

I want to offer my unborn children more than just a chance to be a hashtag.
I want the dreams I have for them to stop being labeled with toe tags.
Stuffed in body bags
Just old rags tossed to the side—
I'm finding out what happens when young, gifted and Black collide.
They can tell me it was just Sandra's time
Or that Eric and Alton were both in the wrong place.
But the real problem is that the enemy removed the hood from his face.
He swapped it out for a badge and a gun,
Traded his horse for a police cruiser
To make the chase a more fun.
Tamir Rice, Philando Castile, Rekia Boyd, Aiyana Stanley-Jones-
They were all precious souls but just prey
When we get down to bare bones.
Kathryn Johnston, Kimani Gray, Sean Bell and Mike Brown
Make you ask if a black body falls under law enforcement,
Does it really make a sound?
Kenneth Chamberlain, Sr., Amadou Diallo, Tavares McGill-
We have been fighting for years but the battle is uphill.
I don't want to keep falling asleep on pillows stained with tears.
I don't want to have to teach my children they should live in fear.
I don't want them to feel like they will be gunned down
If they stand up.
I don't want them to keep seeing us die in the streets with our hands up.
I don't want pain and anger to be all they know.
Stunted flowers without power
With no room to grow.
I write with grit in my pen when there is something on my chest.
Jordan and Trayvon didn't deserve to die either.
But I digress.
"Not guilty" is the mantra when my people die.
All we have left are picket signs when no one tells us why.
Everyone ignores the pieces of the puzzle that don't fit.
Then they hit us with this "All Lives Matter" bullshit.
I'm not saying all lives don't matter.
Let's get that straight.
But it's a scapegoat phrase to divert attention
From the Black lives they take.
We're called angry when we protest after seeing our
Murders on the news.
But honestly how you would feel if you were in
Our shoes?

It's true that everyone in life has their own cross to bear.
We're found guilty from birth just for the skin we wear.
To say "I see people, not color" is a nice scope of humanity at a glance.
But in THIS America,
All lives don't matter and black lives don't stand a chance.
It's open season and we can only pray we don't get caught.
We still don't have a seat at the table
And all we're offered is food for thought.
We can't stay silent.
There is far too much at stake.
Angry, militant, pro-Black-
Call me what you want
But I'm awake.

TK

LOVE ME RIGHT

Love me right and I'll make you immortal.
I'll bronze you or dip you in gold
And make sure people come from miles
Around to admire us both.
Make me smile and I'll give you the prestige
Of lost worlds.
People will forget about Atlantis
Because everyone will want to explore YOU.
Make my heart skip a beat and
I will drape you in silk and
Dip you in diamonds.
You will shine like never before.
Send chills down my spine and I will
Give you the majesty of The Nile.
You can flow strongly and in
Any direction you choose.
Make me warm and fuzzy inside
And I will give you the
Strength of The Alps.
Nothing will ever look stronger next to you.
    Love me wrong and you'll be my Hiroshima.
    All of your beauty will be negated by the bombs I drop.
    Mishandle my heart and become Pompeii.
    I will throw my shawl of ash over you and give you my Vesuvius Stare.
    Make withdrawals from my heart without repayment
    And I will snap my fingers and give you 1929, watch you crash….and burn.
    Fire! Blaze! Watts Riots! Oh yeah, I will give it all to you.
    Lie to me and call me your Trojan Horse
    Because you've granted me entry to wreck you.
    Ignore my feelings and I can make you the Pavlopetri of my life,
    Forgotten, buried and disregarded.
    Either way, I can make you history.
    Just be careful how you love me.

TK

ATM

The little man in the machine
Says I have insufficient funds.
Hell, I didn't need to press any
Buttons to know that.
I knew when I sat down at that
Damn desk and said everything I was told to say
And was called "argumentative and combative"
By those I was supposed to surrender
My power of thought to
That the funds they paid me to do so were INSUFFICIENT.
Every morning I got up and followed their dress code
And spoke in tongues of propaganda
And I knew the reward was INSUFFICIENT.
I knew when I was driving there and my gas hand
Teetered toward "E" and I just prayed to make it
To Friday to get the cash that was already spent
That it was all INSUFFICIENT.
I knew when I opened those bills last week,
Closed my eyes tightly and tried to wish away the zeros
That it was all INSUFFICIENT.
So news flash, Little Man:
You didn't tell me anything I didn't already know.
Now, give me my damn card back.

TK

DISMEMBERED

I cut myself into pieces today.
I sliced open every vein that meant something
And let the blood run out.
I drenched everyone I love with my sanguine affection.
I loved the smiles on their faces just before they went under.
I walked away and went to find the ones I hated.
For them, I cut a special vein on the other side of my heart.
As I bled, I spat words into the puddle that sparked fire
And I reveled at the symphony of its sparks and crackles.
One by one, I pushed them in and watched their hateful
Flesh slide from their bones.
I smiled.
I cut a vein for those I respected too.
I watched as their heads were adorned with revelry.
Then I proceeded to strip off the flesh that defined me.
I stepped out of it and left it heaped upon the floor.
It felt so good to be free of labels and inhibitions.
I peeled apart my bones and built a cage of torture for those
Who threw their stones at me.
I rejoiced in the fear in their eyes.
They feared the newfound me.
I took my heart, my most important piece and buried it
In the sands of time.
I made sure it was a place where no one could find it
And I could never be hurt again.
I stood in a pool of myself,
Dripping with remnants of my past.
I looked at the pieces of me.
How I will enjoy putting them back together.

TK

DAHLIA

I wish to be like her.
Divided.
Heart split from loins,
Love a world away from lust.
They Exist separately now,
But you see they are neighbors.
To have them separated by
A strip of earth, all that is
Organic and good
Would be a dream come true.
To give arousing embraces
Breasts upon breasts
Heartbeat upon heartbeat
Without a single thought resting upon intimacy.
I want to be able to sit next to the man
That I mistakenly love for years,
Let him take me home and
Screw me six ways from Sunday but
NEVER again let him get close to my heart.
To have a face that carries stories
Of the heartless nature of men
Yet to possess beauty that is
Recognized every time you look at me.
To have a past everyone wants to know about and
Fights for a piece of.
To have men come forward and
Accept blame for what was
Done to me, not once
Saying that a moment of it was my fault.
My sex and love both coveted
But lying apart as though
I am a treasure map
With no promise of a prize
But knowing they will still search anyway.
They want me.
Love without Sex,
Sex without Love-
Feeling good about the fact that they can live
As separate beings.
When the man who buys me flowers begins
To expect more,
I will show him fruitless, unpleasing Earth
In place of the cave he hope to enter.
Rather than disappointment,
He will show sympathy and respect for my virtue.

The man who has magic in his hips and
Steel between his thighs will be forced to hear my words
Because having all of me is impossible.
The man who wants my heart will take what I offer
Knowing there is no more to come.
He will look and see that pieces of me
Are gone.
The pieces of me that have been removed might quite
Possibly have become the love and devotion
He desired.
He is sympathetic.
The halves of me lie like two
Marvelous statues on a background
Of fresh green.
I am studied.
I am longed for.
I am loved.
I am intriguing.
An Exquisite Corpse am I.

TK

4 A.M.

It's 4 a.m., Dear Lover.
Now is not the time for you.
This is the time you should be snuggled in the
Arms of the one who makes you giggle and post
All those cheesy pictures online.
You should be lying in bed planning
Your future, complete with six kids
Two dogs and a house.
You should be coming up with all the mean
Things you'll say tomorrow to the single, fucked up girls
Of the world.
Better yet, you should be having the sex you
Allude to only when you bring up the fact that
The rest of us are lonely.
You should be just getting in from the parties
You love that the rest of us weren't invited to.
You should be watching those wedding videos and
Zeroing in on how your friends look so jealous beside
You at the altar.
You should be still expressing your disgust at them
Trying to drink their problems away at the reception.
You should be off somewhere being as happy as you say you are.
So, why is it that you're calling me instead?
Did you suddenly have a bad day with the one
Who will wake up and still love you tomorrow?
Or did you actually remember that you have a friend
Who didn't die right after you said "I do"?
What happened?
Did you find the phone number of an ex in his cell phone?
Did she reply to a text from an old boyfriend?
Did he tell you you've gained weight?
Did she laugh hysterically at a joke her ex-fiancé told?
Or did you remember that you had a friend who stood by
You during all of your breakups?
Did you remember who introduced you?
Or are you calling because I am the only one
You know who's awake?
Or am I supposed to tell you an anecdote from my life
That will make yours seem so much better?
Can't you just go away and let me be as pathetic as you say I am?
Can't you allow me not to be jealous of you for one minute?
Can't you, for a second, not make me feel like everyone has someone
But me?
Can't you spare me the details of how annoyed you will pretend to be
Only to end up putty in each other's hands?

Can't you for ONCE not give me the "Be glad you're single" speech
Right before the gushes and coos about how much you love each other?
Don't even act like you remember me.
Don't try the "Remember when" and "I'm so glad we're friends" game with me.
Please just go away.
It's 4am.
It's the crying hour.
And I really don't want you here.

TK

MAMA SAID

My mama told me love would find me someday.
But I plan to run as fast as my legs will carry me.
I have seen what love does to people
And I want no part of it.
It weakens even the strongest of us.
It forces you out of character and
Frankly, makes you stupid.
It makes you smile for no reason and look like a total asshole
For taunting those who love doesn't love.
I refuse to let love catch me and do to me
What it does to those fools.
I won't let it make me sit by the phone and
Feel empty when it doesn't ring.
I won't let it make me change everything about myself
When I was perfectly fine to begin with.
I won't give all of myself to someone only to have them
Unwrap me, play with me and throw me in a corner.
I won't hurt.
I won't cry.
I won't suffer.
So, sorry Mama.
I have other plans.

TK

HOLLY

Holly got to school early that day.
She just never knew she wouldn't walk away.
One classmate looked depressed and things went wrong
When he flashed the shiny metal gun he'd brought along.
This boy never had much to talk about
But he was heard when all the shots rang out.
Students screamed. Tears began to flow.
Holly should have stayed home, but she just didn't know.
She ran to an empty classroom to hide
But found another gunman already inside.
She knew the face behind the gun.
She sat next to this girl in English 201.
The girl didn't flinch as Holly stared.
She'd taken at least ten lives. Why should Holly's be spared?
Holly's impression on her had not been nice.
But, come on. Everyone had teased her at least once or twice.
The girl looked at Holly and flashed a twisted smile.
She let Holly just stand there and cry for a while.
Holly would regret all the times she laughed at her clothes
And the day she tripped her at lunch and broke her nose.
She'd regret laughing at her glasses and spitting gum in her hair
And loosening the bolts in the seat of her chair.
"Come on, Grace," Holly cried, "You know I was just having some fun
Please. We can talk about this. Please put down the gun."
"I told you you'd be sorry, Holly. But you never did learn.
You've had all of your fun. And now it's my turn."
She raised the barrel to Holly's forehead,
Within an instant, Holly, Cheerleader Captain, was dead.
A weight had been lifted from the center of Grace's chest.
With Holly and her friends gone, they wouldn't hurt anyone else.
She listened to the carnage her fellow outsiders caused in the hall
Then as promised, she aimed at her own chin and ended it all.
As different as "Gross" Grace Conley and Holly Stanton were
When they lay there lifeless, finally, Grace was equal to her.
Holly got to school early that day.
She just never knew she wouldn't walk away.

TK

STRANGE FRUIT

A man was lynched yesterday.
I was states away but someone recorded it for me.
Or maybe they did it for him.
Maybe they wanted there to be evidence of
How he should still be here.
Maybe they wanted there to be proof that he didn't
Do what his killer said he did.
As traumatic as it already was,
That same someone decided to share it with social media.
They gave us all a timeline
Of our brother's final breath.
They knew most of us would never get to meet him
So, they gave us proof he existed.
In that moment, we skipped introductions
And saw him when he was most vulnerable.
We played the whisper game and told our neighbor.
They told theirs and so forth and so on.
But in this version of the game,
The story never changed.
Our brother was suspected of something
That we will never know if he was guilty of.
The offense might have been punishable by
A few years *breathing* behind bars
Or *breathing* on probation
Or *breathing* during community service
Or *breathing* while paying a fine
Or *breathing* deeply during a trial.
But all of those breaths were nullified when
Someone decided they were just not equitable enough.
Him breathing while paying his debt to society
Somehow would have made their pockets
A little lighter or taken years off their lives.
That had to be the case because they were so
Against him breathing.
Why else would they have taken him?
The people who are supposed to be sworn
To protect and serve
And other human beings who bleed the same
Couldn't be racist, right?
There is no way that they took our brother
Just because his skin was darker.
They couldn't have decided that because of his dark skin,
His life didn't matter.

They couldn't have thought no one would
Mourn him, miss him or be angry.
They couldn't have thought of him as one less
Fly in the milk and considered what they did
A service to God and country because
That would have been inhumane.
Right?
Their outrage at our outrage has to be because
They had a good reason.
Maybe they feel because we only came to know
Him in his final moments, we missed the kill or be killed
Ultimatum he gave them.
Maybe we missed the ceremony right after where
They were deemed judge, jury and executioner.
Or maybe they think we are being irrational and
Not doing our due diligence to find the importance
Of the candy bar he stole when he was four or
The test he cheated on in junior high.
I can only speculate.
But what I know for sure is that
A man was lynched yesterday
And I am mad as hell about it.

TK

ONCE UPON A TIME

Take off your hood and bed sheet.
Let me see your face.
Be proud to be responsible for all that
Is taking place.
Be bold enough to tell me you don't care about my sons.
Rather than pull any strings for them,
You would rather pull your guns.
Be open and say you'd rather see us all
Swinging from your ropes.
After all, how dare we have the audacity to hope.
To hell with all our dreams.
We've been nothing but a stain on the country
Or so it seems.
There seems to be no greater curse than to be born brown.
But let me hip you to history.
Shut your mouth and gather 'round.
"Once upon a time we were kings and queens" would be gross and understated.
Now our culture is one to be cherry picked and appropriated.
There was a time we built kingdoms through hard work
But now there is more merit in how many we teach to twerk.
Intentional hours in the sun give others the hue of our natural skin
But give us no volunteers to join the situations we're in.
At one point, our Hottentot-like features were viewed as ugly and obscene.
But now I see y'all flaunting them on the covers of magazines.
I have no problem with white girls flirting and twerking for Instagram.
But I take issue with those who label me as anything less than the queen I am.
Cornrows were ugly when you saw them paired with black skin.
But put them on you, call them "boxer braids" and suddenly they are what's in.
Full lips and thick hips weren't anything you could see for yourselves.
Now you're picking them out and trying them on like items on a shelf.
My beauty ain't no grocery store.
Make sure you get that right.
Don't just sift through, squeeze and pinch to try and choose what's ripe.
You can NEVER wear my Black like me.
But it's cute of you to try.
My magic has no substitute, despite what money can buy.
The majesty of my brothas is unbridled and unmatched.
My kings have missed their crowns for a while but I'm
Glad they're taking them back.
The lines about us in history books have long been written in invisible ink.
But it's beautiful when we go looking for them, start to wake up and think.
Our people didn't always cower under the cracks of whips.
We were the mothers and fathers of the earth before we got on those ships.
I don't want you to hide the fact that you think we are less than you
Say it to our faces like you "red-blooded Americans do".

We've already heard that "If you don't like our country, leave" bit.
But you stole it from the Natives and Black brawn helped grow this shit.
We are taking back our strength
In hopes that all oppression will end.
But we need you out in the open
Before we make the mistake of calling you friends.
We're strong.
We're Black.
We're proud and intelligent to boot.
You may not fully understand where we came from.
But you will respect our roots.

TK

YOU'RE HERE

If you'll excuse me,
I just wanna lie here and bask in you.
I know that physically,
You aren't with me.
But you're everywhere.
You're the joy that walks through
My front door in the morning.
You're the cool that rests
On my couch.
You're the calm that lays next to me
In bed at night.
And I
Have never felt more at home.

TK

THROUGH THE LOOKING GLASS

Yesterday, I heard a knock from my mirror. I'm still not sure about answering. I have to admit that it frightened me a bit. I know exactly who knocked. I have seen her before but I'm not sure if I can trust her yet. She looks like me. Almost exactly. But she is still completely different. Her shoulders don't slump. Her skin shines brighter. There is pain in her eyes but I can see little bits of joy peeking through. She has a smile that she doesn't just wear for pictures. It says there is something that she is actually happy about. She still has my booty but her stomach is flat the way I wish mine was again. Even though there is no music, she is dancing—hands up in the air, eyes closed, hips swaying slowly—a dance I have no clue how to do. She is one of the happiest people I have ever seen. I don't think I know her well enough to trust her yet but she intrigues me. She's busy with her joy right now. But if she knocks again today, maybe I will invite her out here to join me. I could stand to know her.

TK

LADY ON THE BENCH

My Sista,

Let me start by saying "I'm sorry". The blisters on your feet tell me the last thing you want to do is go 'round and 'round with me. This day has been long but still not as long as the nights you have spent crying with only your own arms to hold you. All the while, you are just wondering if he is going to come home. The rain fell hard today, but not as hard as the impact of the task of raising your son alone and free from his father's flaws. I see you staring at your umbrella as you wonder why it can't shield you from the emotional rain that falls. You wonder when someone or something will shield and protect the *whole* you. You resent that jacket for letting the bitter cold of the world break through. You hate your shoes because through them, you can still feel the burn of the tight rope you walk just to keep the lights on and food on the table. You look with pity upon your pants because all day, your boss makes it clear that he wonders what's in them. Your blouse is your worst enemy because your heart wants to beat out loud but remains confined. More often than ever, you just want to stand naked and free and yell to the world, "This is me! Can you see me now?!" You wonder if even then they will see what you're going through. I know. I won't take up too much of your time. But I just want to say that I understand.

TK

I'M IN LOVE

I'm in love with you, Love.
And I don't think that's a bad thing.
You make me feel better than anyone or anything ever has before.
It's you and not them that makes all the bad things disappear.
It's you who has me walking around with my head in the clouds.
It's you who kisses me softly and paints my mind all types of beautiful.
It's you who lies with me and makes me feel like a queen.
It's you who takes control of my body and makes me want you more.
It's you who makes my heart swell with joy.

> It isn't until people disrespect you
> That you start kicking ass and taking names.
> It isn't until they treat you like you're less than
> That you bring tears to their eyes and pain to their hearts.
> It's not until they ignore you
> That you disturb their minds and not give them a moment's rest.
> It's not until they curse you
> That you slap the tastes out of their mouths.
> It's not until they don't recognize your power
> That you have to show them who's boss.
> But I like that.
> I think it's kinda sexy.

I have been in love with you for quite some time
But I haven't wanted to admit it.
All I saw was the pain and disappointment
That always seemed to show up whenever you did.
All I saw was people getting hurt
Every time you crossed their paths.
I thought you were bad news.
So I smiled at you coyly from a distance.
But I always wondered how it would be if you

And I were one.
I wondered how it would feel
To be wrapped in your arms.
I wondered how it would feel
To walk into a room with you on my arm.
I wondered how it would feel
To be that girl all the other girls envied.
But I was too scared to speak up.

>I've wised up, Love.
>I'll tell anyone I love you now.
>Especially since I know
>You don't love me any less than you loved the rest.
>I'm in love with you, Love.
>And I have to admit,
>It feels good.

TK

IN PASSING

When I told her she was beautiful,

My face remained the same.

When I said I liked her shoes,

My own remained unchanged.

When I said I liked her hair,

Mine still stayed in place.

When I said I liked her brows and lashes,

Mine stayed on my face.

When I said, "Girl, I love that top,"

Mine stayed on my back.

When I complimented her lipstick,

Mine still stayed in tact.

When I said I liked her purse,

My money stayed in mine.

When I said her skin was beautiful,

My own remained just fine.

I see no real point in competing

With that next girl.

She should not be my enemy,

But my ally in this world.

I choose to compliment her

And build her up even more.

Each time I do,

I remain just as ravishing as before.

TK

What is the strangest compliment you have given or been given to a total stranger? What was the reaction?

___
___
___
___
___
___
___
___
___

THE VEIN

Let me be your Betsy Blair.
Take my hand, be my Gene Kelly
And let's dance a routine across the floor
Of every heart that happens upon us.
Let's show them love in motion.
I want to be the Yoko to your John
Because I feel inspired and I want you to
Feel that way too.
So, like she did, let me sew my
Spirit to yours
And as we wrap our arms around the
Shoulders of others,
We will stitch a quilt of peace, love and acceptance.
I can be the Lucy to your Desi
And throw a shawl of laughter over us when
The world turns cold with oppression.
It's funny to me that it doesn't matter
Whether I am the Gwen or Fredrika
To your Huey because either way
The power of your revolution will
Ebb and flow within me and bring new
Life to a generation that will rule the world
With a fist held high.
I want to be the Cicely to your Miles
And keep burning the fires of affection that the
Snuffers of time cannot put out.
Let me bathe in your loving mixture of Blue in Green.
Let me be the spice in your Bitches Brew.
We need that Ossie and Ruby Dee love
That does not need to be spoken
But with one look in our eyes, the world
Knows that both it AND we are unmoving and unbreakable.
Please understand that by being the
Betty to your Malcolm
I become the mothering hand that spoons
Vigor onto the plates of children seeking
Peaceful means of protest.
I seek not to be a new form of romance to you
But an antique love
Preserved with the polish of wisdom
And devoid of devotional dust.
I seek to be that love you have read about
But have never seen.

The kind that is rooted in history,
Grown from authenticity and
Stretches its limbs over cliffs
To provide shade from all that is untrue.
I seek to be what is vital and
Makes its role known without parting its lips.
I seek to be love's vein.

TK

YOU

My mother always told me

If I have nothing nice to say,

I should refrain from saying anything

At all.

Therefore, never again,

Will I speak of you.

TK

SOMEONE YOU USED TO KNOW

Allow me to apologize for who I was when you knew me.
During the time I was loving you,
I wasn't making much time to love myself.
I hung on that notion that you are were somehow a reflection of me and
If I loved you enough, I would somehow get what I needed.
I was wrong.
I filled myself with hope every day and wrapped my arms around you to share it.
I mistook that sharp pain in my side for rough edges of the cuts
You had that I was helping to heal.
I didn't notice the knife you had stuck into me
Or that everything was draining from me.
One day I got sick of being stupid and decided to wake up.
At some point, I stretched my limbs too far and ended up shaking you right off.
As I wiped sleep from my eyes, I managed to wipe away all images of you too.
So, as a friend, you can say, "Yeah. We used to be cool, but…"
As an ex-lover, you can say, "Yeah. Been there. Done that."
You were there for the life of the coal.
It's only fair that you are at a distance
Now that the diamond has finally learned to shine.

TK

YOUR TRUTH

I love your version of the truth.
Come closer so I can see all the colors.
Tell me that part again about
How I'm always wrong and you're always right.
I never get tired of hearing it.
Or how about the part that
Gave you a reason to walk away.
I love hearing about how you were
"Just scared and confused".
One more time, go back to the
Part where you say I think
I'm better than you.
Nobody says that the way you do.
Better yet, repeat the part about
How I always wanted more than you
Could ever give?
Now THAT is priceless.
I love the way you throw
Decorations on the details
And drape fantasy around the facts.
In your version of the story, I wear the horns
And I am not even fit to shine your halo.
Your version of events are like none
I have ever heard.
Now, I would never call you a liar.
I believe you just tell the truth
In a much different color than most.
You never have to convince me.
As long as you believe you
And you can sleep at night,
That's really all that matters.

TK

THE PRENUP

America wants a divorce. To be honest, she asked for one a long time ago. But we stayed, thinking that if we fought hard enough, we could work things out. From the beginning, we've had our spats and I'm sure it had to do with the nefarious nature of her vows. She said, "...all men are created equal" and "...with liberty and justice for all". But she never had us in mind. However as time passed and we began to define ourselves, we wrote ourselves into the "all men" and "for all" portions. Every now and then she reminds us that she never loved us and we weren't included in those words. So, there is always a point of contention. We've stayed at odds and our issues have bubbled quietly below the surface. But America always made it clear that she would rather be married to anyone BUT us. She degraded us, called us names and killed off parts of us every day. To those vows she wrote, she took her quill dipped in our blood and added "By the way, I called you property when we met so this doesn't really apply to you". Just recently, we had another fight and enough was enough. But in America's greatest error, she didn't make her edits official. As in any divorce, friends chose sides. America didn't expect any of the friends who looked like her to choose us or to believe we weren't the monster she made us out to be. She never thought we would point out the fact that she started with nothing and we gave her nearly everything she has. She can marvel at beautiful buildings because we built them. She can boast an economy because we invest. She can grow her food because we once tended the soil. She can function because we dared to be innovative. She expected for us to go away quietly. But we decided to fight. Because we built everything without payment, the property decided to OWN property. And we teeter back and forth between lighting matches and marching for it. America yells her disapproval as she watched the flames but we refuse to hear her until she stops feeling like we deserve to die new deaths and that our existence is less valuable than what we have set ablaze. We will not be silenced. We will not leave until we get our half.

TK

BAGGAGE CLAIM

Yeah. I have baggage.
But who bought it for me?
There is no way I would have asked
To have these extra things hanging off of me.
I mean, this shit is heavy.
Maybe it would be easier for me to
Check it if you had paid any part of the price.
Instead you used my currency.
My sweat,
My tears,
My peace,
My heart.
Now I'm standing here at this counter
Looking dumb and broke (n).
Everyone else runs past me and
Makes their flights to joy.
I feel I may never be cleared for takeoff.

TK

SO SORRY

Somebody made a mistake.
Somebody forgot to fall in love with you.
It's possible that it's someone you met only once.
Maybe you talked for ten seconds about how great a party was
And then went to opposite corners of the dance floor when your
Favorite songs came on.
Or maybe you smiled at each other once before a movie
But thought the only things that could have come of talking
Would have been an awkward moment and cold popcorn.
And NOBODY likes cold popcorn.
Even worse, maybe it's someone you've known for years.
Maybe the two of you were in grade school together and
Graduated from finger paints to college acceptance letters
And didn't bother to have that kiss in between.
Or maybe you knew each other from the
Neighborhood you grew up in but instead of asking
Your name, they were content to be that familiar passerby.
I don't know who it was or what their reason,
But SOMEBODY dropped the ball.
It's because of them that you haven't been
Given the world
And that you have to sit back and watch the ways those
Who don't even deserve a pinch of paradise undermine
What they have.
It's all this careless person's fault that you lie alone
At night with your mind racing when you are
Supposed to have someone to share those thoughts with.
It's because of them that the love you deserve
Has yet to find you.
It's true that it's their mistake.
But you have my sincerest apology.

TK

THEORY ON SATURN

I have a theory about Saturn. For all the other silly planets, their migrations are a chore. For her, they are victory laps. She moves slowly and with intent so that everyone sees her. Her rings are for show. They are trophies from her conquests and it is all those who know her name can talk about. She has her own moons and that's something to brag about. She can. But she doesn't. She's far more graceful than that. She has her own clouds. And as much joy as she brings lovers who see her, no one is fit to walk upon them. She is much too precious for that. Oh and that Great White Spot she gets from time to time is just a quick reminder of her power. While people are talking about who is from Venus and Mars, she will not be ignored. Saturn is a constant reminder of class from the heavens. She hopes that we will decide to take notes and someday adapt her wonder for ourselves.

TK

Photo by Reggie Raphael Wallace

U.B. (UNAPOLOGETICALLY BLACK)

Fist held high,
Afro perfectly round,
Skin the color of a bar of chocolate-
I'm not sorry.

I *hear* the thunder in Malcolm's voice
And I *feel* the thunder in the ideas of Martin.
Huey speaks my mind.
Stokely sings my soul-
And I'm not sorry.

Angela is my spirit animal.
I growl with the vigor of Nina.
But I dance with the grace of Maya-
And I am not sorry.

I'm strong like Assata.
I'm powerful like Betty.
I'm virtuous like Coretta.
I am ingenious like Sonia-
And I am not sorry.

I live in Erykah's soulful moans.
I revel in the rim shots of Questlove.
A hot 16 from Talib gives me wings.
K Dot lights a fire in me-
And I am not sorry.

I speak my mind the way 3 Stacks does.
I sing my roots just like India.
I put my story on the big screen like Ava -
And I am not sorry.

I'm mad about Ferguson.
I'm angry about the Central Park Five.
The Jena 6 and The Edmund Pettus Bridge still furl my brow.
I will never forget the blood of Rumain Brisbon
Of Akai Gurley
Of Tyree Woodson
Of Victor White III
Of Yvette Smith
Of Jordan Davis

Of Jonathan Ferrell
Of Kimani Gray
Of Chavis Carter
Of Rekia Boyd
Of Trayvon Martin
Of Oscar Grant
Of Tamir Rice
Of Eric Garner
Of Sandra Bland
Of Philando Castile

And I am not sorry.

TK

TICKET TO RIDE

Excuse me.
I think I've missed my flight to Perfection.
It says right here on my ticket that I should have boarded by
By 0300.
And since it is supposed to be a short flight, I should arrive
No later than 0350.
I know I am a little late.
I don't know if it's because I stopped to pack all those extras
Or because I allowed too many distractions as I was on the way here,
But I am running behind.
I'm pretty sure everyone else who actually made the flight
Would say I didn't need these things so they couldn't
Possibly understand my reason for having to go back and get them.
You see, I know that my husband and children are
Waiting for me in Perfection.
But I needed a few things before I saw them.
I wanted to be sure not to do them the disservice of coming empty-handed.
I have a career waiting there too.
That I will DEFINITELY need to be prepared for.
I spent my time stitching a nice thick coat for the bitter cold
I will face on the journey to it.
I'm staring at the board as all the times and destinations change.
I see the smiles on the faces of everyone as they make their connections.
I know that I got here a little after my flight tine
But I am still determined to reach Perfection.
It wasn't in my plan to take a later flight.
But I will do whatever it takes.
So, if you will kindly rebook me on the next flight out,
I will greatly appreciate it.

TK

DON'T STOP DANCING

Don't stop dancing.
Give yourself a gift each day
As you pirouette towards success.
Love yourself a little more
As you tap upon greatness.
Smile a little bigger
When you twirl into joy.

TK

MARRY ME TOMORROW

Marry me tomorrow.
When I say that, don't take it to mean that I am not madly in love with you at this moment.
It's just that when we started this whole thing, I told you divorce was never my goal.
I told you it was never in my plan to end up hating the person I have loved more than anyone
I have ever met.
But if we do this now,
I'm afraid it's inevitable.
You see, there are some things you aren't quite done with
That won't let it work right now.
You aren't done partying until you see the sun
Getting so drunk and high you forget the fun
Bathing strippers in stacks of ones--
But I'm not judging you.
You still wanna be in the club every night
And expect me to say that's alright.
Someday, I'm sure you'll see the light --
But I'm not rushing you.
You explain every argument with "Oh, she's crazy",
Think I'm good enough to have your babies
Yet refuse to call me your lady--
But I'm not pushing you.
You still think that I don't see
How you look at other women when you're with me
But God forbid another man sees me--
But I'm not dissecting you.
I can't lie and say I didn't get a little sentimental
When you dropped to one knee in
Front of all our family and friends.
You did it the way you saw it done in the movies.
You're a quick study.
But I need to be sure this hand in mine
Will only meet my cheek to caress it,
That it will be there each night to rock
Our babies to sleep
And that we are the only ones to benefit from its touch.
I'm madly in love with you now.
But I'm not sure you're thinking clearly.
So I will let you keep this ring
Until you get everything out of your system that doesn't belong there.
Ask me when it's all over.
By then, I'm sure it will fit perfectly.

TK

INTERGALACTIC

Let me hitch a ride to Neptune.
I bet I could if I stared at you long enough.
Just seeing your face takes me places
The astronauts would beg to explore.
Your touch has me tap dancing on dust clouds
And Baby, I love the way it feels.
We make marks on Jupiter
The world will wonder about for years to come.
When we love, it's like
We scoop up fists full of the sun
And drink them down smoothly.
Please believe it's hot.
You bring me down slowly and lay me
On moonbeams.
We rest slightly above Earth.
We wouldn't dream of coming down.

TK

FORBIDDEN WORDS

Things have been completely upside down since you left. I have been walking on stormy skies and hitting my head on the ground with each stride. Rational thoughts are things of the past and I never get very far with all this damn rain in my shoes. Never mind the sunshine everyone else is seeing. From this angle, everything is just a blur anyway. Or maybe it's the fact that all the blood has rushed to my head giving me food for overthought. I spend a lot of time on the "What If He" and not enough on the "How Can We". I know it's stupid. But I can't help it. We were even less than two ships passing in the night. As far as love goes, we were more like two shores that would never meet. But nowadays, I feel like I'm drowning without you. I'm not even sure if it was a simple gesture or just hearing your voice on the line that had me transfixed, but I have been in this stupor over you for quite a while now. I'm not sure when I became stupid over you. But I know that first kiss taught me all I needed to know. I can't say I love you because that makes me sound desperate. After all, it was you who folded and packed up all the love and I would lose my dignity if I crawled after you and begged for you to leave a stitch behind for me. I can't say that I miss you because by now I should be able to stand on my own two feet and be a whole me the way I was before I met you. So instead I will remain silent. I will trek in confusion and let the clouds of the past wrap around me and pray that your memory loosens its grip.

TK

PERFECT STRANGER

I wonder where you are right now. Are you thinking of me? I think this sudden tingle across my face is the feeling of your mind on me. But I don't want to assume. I don't really know who you are but I have loved you for years. Only recently, have I subscribed to the idea that you might be feeling the same. Most of my days, I am pretty comfortable with the thought of loving you and waiting until we cross paths. But sometimes I lie awake wondering if you are coping well with the stress of the day and the guilt arises because I am not there to hold you. On birthdays, I graciously accept gifts from others but feel like an ingrate because all I really want is to be with you. I don't know about you. But during family gatherings, I can't help looking around a crowded room and then feeling the empty space next to me where you should be. I am proud of the fact that you have your successes, but I always pray that you are not giving up on me. I often wonder if we are making the same mistakes at the same time in the frustration of waiting. I wonder if you too are dating others and making a mental list of all the ways in which they fall short of being me. Do you give them the halfhearted smiles and laughs knowing that you are saving the real ones for me? Do you wish them away the morning after and close your eyes tightly imaging I am there? When you have the best or worst days, do you rush home to tell me about them? When you look around and realize I am not there, does your heart still break? Do you still write down your dreams for us in hopes that we will come together someday and compare notes? Do you hear the laughter of our children and let it warm you from within? Are there times you are surrounded by friends but you find that no adventure or conversation means much because you aren't sharing it with me? Do you ever find it funny that you have so much going on in life, but know within your heart of hearts that the day you will finally begin to live is the day I am in your arms. Sometimes I just wonder.

TK

GLASS HOUSES

"People in glass houses shouldn't throw stones."
We hear it all the time.
But no one ever has any advice about what to do when you
Become the glass house-
When you can't even begin to think of criticizing others
Because you can't hide any of your own dirty laundry.
You don't wear your heart on your sleeve but instead
Become a full suit of yourself.
You're sensitive to touch and depending on how the wind blows,
You can be tipped and swayed to the point where something inside
Of you falls off a shelf and everything falls apart.
There is no point in locking the doors because everyone who sits on
Your lawn has a front row seat to your fears and pain.
They see your soul when it stands at the top of the staircase
And when it takes that wrong step and stumbles to the bottom.
They see all the cracks in your foundation and what years of
Storms have done to you.
But rather than placing a survival kit on your doorstep,
You see them palming the same dirty stones behind their backs
You could have sworn everyone knew not to throw.
It's too good to be true that we all learned the same lesson.
The only thing you can do is pray that when each stone hits you,
The damage is minimal and that your pleas for less transparent
Walls will be heard.
You can only hope to no longer be on display.

TK

MICHELLE,

You are a hero to me even when I don't deserve you. During the times I feel it might be karmatic for me to go low when they do, I see how graceful you look when you go high and I want that for myself. You always look proud to stand by your man but you are proof that doing so does not mean you cannot sustain on your own. When you look at your daughters, your eyes are filled with assurance, hope and unmitigated pride in the women you know they will become.

I knew my skin tone was powerful before I knew who you were. But I never knew my melanin was magical enough to mesmerize those who have it not. YOU taught me that, Mrs. O. The whole world fell in love with you not because of the trophy you felt you had to be but because you are always comfortable being the educated girl from the Southside of Chicago who can uphold you with the law but cut you down with a mean side eye if she has to. Whether you were meeting the queen, dancing with Beyonce or talking history with Oprah, you always stayed true. You never filled my ears with talk of silver spoons that you never owned and ever when you could afford one, you always stressed to me the importance of feeding others- be it literally or just food for thought. You boldly spoke about your children playing on the lawn of a home that was built by slaves and when you knew your words bit, you stood firmly in their truth. It was a relief to see someone who looked like she could be my mother's sister or at least a play cousin looking dignified at the heads of tables that historically would not have been set for her. You are that secret supernova. You came out of nowhere to show little Black girls who were rejected and downtrodden that they could stay Black and still be successful. We didn't know you would shine the way you do but we are all touched by your light. I don't love you BECAUSE you're Black. But I would be lying if I said it doesn't make me open my arms a little wider to you.

I know you hurt sometimes. I can only imagine the fight against the urge to retaliate when you are mocked and called everything but the well-deserved title of First Lady. Having to hold it together for your family when a large section of ignorant America laughs and cracks jokes at the expense of your family can't be easy. There are nights I'm sure you cry into your pillow not wanting others to bear witness to your tears. But having to put on a happy face when you had no strength, I'm sure, sent your hurt echoing down the hallways. I can't imagine the pressure you felt to turn your wails into melodies and sing the praises of a country that repeatedly betrays your ancestors. You are free from it now, Dear First Lady. And I know that your freedom means a great deal. Now you can dance when you want to. You can cook a meal in your own kitchen and be free to walk down the street. You get those parts of your life back that you, over the last 8 years, have taught the rest of us to appreciate more. I get it. You've done your time there and it is time to move on. But please understand that there is an unremitting ache in the depths of my heart at the thought of seeing you go. For me, you are Lady Liberty. You are all that this country should stand for. I never saw it until you arrived and for me, 8 years is just not long enough. But as with all beautiful birds, if you want them to survive in this world, you have to let them fly. So with that said, with a heavy and aching heart, I watch you soar. But with a determined and vigilant mind that I, too, can touch the sky.

Sincerely,

TK Long

NOVEMBER 8, 2016

We died today, America.
We stood amongst one another and perished.
Even if the causes were different, we all met our ends.
For some of us, it was a death that began months ago
With the rotting of our moral fibers.
But we never took notice of the stench of what was festering inside of us.
Instead, we celebrated strength in numbers when we found out
Others were decaying just as rapidly as we.
Instead of injecting the cure at the site and starting to heal,
We succumbed to the disease.
Racism, sexism and xenophobia make a deadly cocktail
And we were doomed from the first sip.
Some of us died more horrifically and in much larger number.
Our bloodlines drew outlines of our stolen souls in the streets.
We were told to build bridges and extend olive branches
To those who had no real desire to reach us
And we were given only the dead bodies of our loved ones to use as material.
But rather than being allowed to question our causes of death
And assert that our lives matter,
It was decided that we should be permanently silenced.
Maybe someday, there will be a Lazarus effect and we will
Breathe again and return to our former selves.
But for now, we carry on.
The undead-
Roaming the earth in search of our souls.

K

Photo by Reggie Raphael Wallace

I DON'T WANT TO WRITE

Sometimes I sit and think about you.

I don't speak.

I don't write anything down.

I just let you play inside my mind.

I let you tickle the hypotheses of us and

Caress our could be.

I can feel your breath all over my theories.

You give my "just waits" the sweetest kisses.

There are times that I don't want to write about you.

Sometimes I just want you…here.

TK

BARE

I am most beautiful when I let go.

During the times I throw up my hands

And let it all fall, I glow.

The heaviness hits the ground and shatters.

Shards fly

But I relish in the fact that

They are down there, and I am up here.

No inhibitions cloak my joy.

No indifference clouds my peace.

No intolerance veils my being.

I am most perfect

When I am laid bare.

TK

NINA IN VARIATION

I am Nina in variation.
I am what suits you.

In the times you are at war,
I am the Simone sort-
A beautiful revolutionary
Colored with complexity.
I'm never afraid to speak my mind
Because I have the power to make
Whatever I say sound like music.
If I lash out at you, it is only because
Of my passion and the things
We are both still working to understand about me.
I'm just a soul whose intentions are good.
Love me anyway.
You won't regret it.

When you want peace,
I am of the Mosley mindset.
I am your muse when you don't
Even know you need one.
I am that silent whisper that pushes past
Your manhood and exposes you.
I mean, the *real* you.
With me, there is no on-stage persona
Hidden behind the paint of pretty words.
I am the last to make love to you
But the first to strip you bare.
I let you be the blues in my left thigh
Knowing you will crave the funk in my right.
When you meet yourself through me,
But still don't understand,
Love me anyway.
You won't regret it.

I am steel.
I am that thing you hold in your hands
That makes you realize the power
Of life and death.

I give you the rush of knowing
You have the strength to kill
But when the sun catches me just right,
You no longer want to.
The curves of my body gleam brightly
And leave you entranced.
You ponder the ingenuity it took to create me.
I'm heavy in your hands.
But your heart and mind are lighter
Knowing that I am here if you ever need me.
When others misuse me
And diminish my beauty,
Love me anyway.
You won't regret it.

I exist in many forms
But always perfectly.

I am a magnificent masterpiece.
I am all you will ever need.

TK

PURPLE HEART

There's a war going on inside of you.

I want nothing more than to help you wage it.

I want to charge into battle with you

And join in on your battle cry.

I want to feel the metal of the enemy's sword.

I want to be able to bleed for you.

You are so battered already.

I want to be the one you can lean on

And limp away with, bearing a victorious smile.

I would cheer loudest when they pin on your medal

And give you a few badges of my own.

You are the bravest soldier I know.

I would be honored to fight beside you.

But I am ill-equipped and I can't come with you.

With my deepest regret, I must let you go alone.

But with outstretched arms,

I will be waiting here when you make it home.

TK

REAL LOVE

Real Love is on life support.

It took a nasty fall from its pedestal,

Which is ironic because

PEOPLE used to fall into IT.

It is lying in a hospital that is busy with people

Running crazy to breathe life into everything that doesn't matter.

Fame gets the antibiotics Real Love needs.

The splints are put on Skin Deep Beauty.

Money gets the bandages.

Sex gets the sutures.

Casts go on Vicious Cycles to hold in their vitality.

Gurneys race down the halls ushering in new insignificant patients.

Tears are shed at their bedsides and people stop at nothing

To keep them all alive.

But Real Love gets no visitors.

It lies alone, busted and bruised,

Ignored,

Clinging to life.

TK

BLACK CHILD

Black Child, I want to invite you to love yourself.
I mean, I'm going to.
So, you might as well join me.
I'm going to adore the way your skin is that shade of brown
That fits perfectly between your mama's and your daddy's.
It's almost like they waited for years for you to come along
And fill that empty bit of canvas that already held a pretty picture.
I'm going to love the kinks and coils of your hair
And how some days, it just doesn't know the meaning of gravity.
I'm going to love watching wiry limbs that don't know what
To do with themselves suddenly become Double Dutch acrobats.
I'm going to love the smiles that spread across your thick lips
As Miss Mary Mack and her silver buttons are given life
With the rhythm from your hands.
I'm going to love you on makeshift basketball courts
Where your passion for the game is the reason you know
That if you cuss about it a little, ain't nobody gon' tell.
I'm going to love you when you're on the corner.
I know you don't skip school because you're dumb.
It is just taking you a while to learn that all easy money ain't good money.
When you sell your body, I know you only do it because
No one has ever truly shown you what you're worth.
If you only knew, you would know that any price is beneath you.
I'm going to love you from the halls of high school to Harvard.
Some think you won't make it there, but I believe in you.
I already know why I love you and why I always will.
In a world that gives you every reason to hate yourself, love is what you need most.
And it might as well start with you and me.

TK

I HATE U

I have never hated you more than
I do for the way you made me love you
Five minutes ago.
Don't get me wrong.
I fall for you every day
But the falling should stop once I decide to be angry.
I really thought I was ready this time.
I had that fold-my-arms-and-turn-my-head-
Don't-laugh-at-any-of-his-jokes-or-caress-his-cheek-
Let-alone-kiss-him
Act down pat.
Then you went and said something sweet and wrecked the whole thing.
Now I'm sitting here hating you but
With a bigger problem on my hands
Because I can't decide if I hate myself
More than I hate you because I fell for
Your sweet shit when I was supposed to be cool.
I'm really not sure you're worth
This kind of trouble.
I'm enjoying this radio silence though.
I needed this time alone with
My thoughts.
Let me enjoy them while I can.
Pretty soon that phone will ring.
And I will have to start hating you
All over again.

TK

LOVE SONG

I'm doing something different this time.

This time, I'm writing a love song for myself.

I'm saving the most beautiful notes I have ever heard for ME.

There are some in there that will make me cry.

But I will love and embrace myself afterward and

All will be well.

I don't have to worry about sticking to a format or

Be concerned that it is too long for listening.

With this song, the longer the better.

The instruments will move me,

But the lyrics hold the power.

These are all the things I will say to myself on

The days I feel low.

These words will be putty for all the cracks in my heart.

Some cracks, I will admit are self-inflicted.

They come from loving too hard when others love too little.

But I won't feel bad for that.

Only healing will matter once the music starts.

There will be a special verse for days like this

When my mind lingers on someone who has made me a mere afterthought.

You know.

When I have loved only to have it

Thrown back in my face.

He may have mattered to me for years.

But I will hum my tune all day and he won't matter by morning.

There will be a verse for friends.

I will sing the love of those who are devout and

Give those who are not their long-awaited benediction.

I will ask that they go with God because they

Are no longer invited to go with me.

My family will get a verse too.

As plentiful as we are,

I am one of a kind.

I have been told I have a face similar to my mother's

And a demeanor similar to my brother's

But my spirit is all my own.

I will sing praises to only those who respect that.

The longest verse will be for me.

That dreamer,

That wild hearted lover,

That sensitive soul that has been hardened by time,

That girl who is angry at the world often but

Rarely admits it because she has been told it is wrong

That girl who is sick of being told what is wrong

Or that *she* is wrong

That girl who stands naked in the mirror with

Dents and dimples and a belly bigger than it was a decade ago

And searches for a reason to love herself,

That girl who is tired but may never show it,

That girl who cries herself to sleep sometimes

But can make you wonder if she ever feels sad at all,

That broken girl who still has some honest smiles left,

That girl who is most beautiful when she loves freely

And is attempting to trust enough to do so again,

That girl who is not perfect but is worth every

Second invested in her,

That girl who is becoming.

My verse is one I will probably play on a loop.

The truth is, I may be perfecting it for the rest of my life.

I will be working on my love song to myself for a while

But that won't stop me from singing it anyway.

After all, practice makes perfect.

I have to get this right though.

From now on,

It is the only song I will ever sing.

TK

BURNED

I'm not sure what you're looking for in my eyes.

But you won't find the fire I used to have.

That was snuffed out when you didn't love me.

You got most of it the first time.

But when I was foolish enough to love you again,

The rest died.

I would like to say that it left my humanity unscathed.

But that's a lie.

It scorched my sensitivity and

Bore holes through my joy.

It spread to my Give-A-Shit and

Melted off its face.

It was useless after that so I decided to throw it out.

My trust was permanently damaged too

After my own raging wildfire ran free.

After your wrath, you couldn't possibly think

I'd be the same.

I should have believed you wanted to be better for me

But I always knew the truth.

My spirit has had its trial by fire.

Please look away so that I can save

What little of me is not yet ash.

TK .

LET LOVE RULE

I hope love happens to you.

I mean that scary, crazy, don't-know-what-to-do kind of love.

In the middle of the night, I want you to lie there

Awake and smiling like a fool.

At the times your "one" is not with you,

I want you to feel lost and empty.

When they tell you a joke,

I want those deep belly laughs for you—

The ones that grow from seeds planted in your soul and

Push past the darkness.

When they tell you their secrets,

I want you to be able to see the doors open and

I want you to run wild as you explore what is behind them all.

When they tell you they don't love you anymore,

I want you to be broken and cry until you're exhausted.

When they beg your forgiveness and tell you they don't mean it,

I want you to breathe that sigh of relief and

Fall into their arms.

I want you so consumed with emotion that you can't breathe.

I wish for love to rule you.

TK

THE SHIT

Today, I realized that I am the shit.

It took a little time.

Last night, I laid down

With the weight of the world on my mind.

But I met myself in my subconscious

While I was asleep.

I forced myself to look at myself and to really dig deep.

My heart was heavier than my eyes and I was a bit of a mess.

But I woke up happy and free today and feeling my absolute best.

I looked at my heart

And realized it was kind.

Despite all it has seen,

There is love left inside.

I thought about how my mind works

And the corners it bends.

I thought about what I do with my gifts and all the hearts

I hope to mend.

I thought about my friends,

Even though these days, they are few.

I'm blessed that such beautiful people

Stuck around to help me through.

I thought of those who hurt me and

All the pain I thought would last.

I thought about the courage it took to

Leave them all in the past.

I fixed my breaking heart

And checked my emotions at today's door.

What had my heart so heavy

Really doesn't matter anymore.

We all have those rough days

Where nothing seems to go our way.

But today, I feel like I'm the shit.

And I hope tomorrow is your day.

TK

What makes you "The Shit"? (Go ahead! BRAG!)

HER (AT THE AIRPORT)

At first, I just liked her boots. But that was before I saw her—large eyes of an icy blue shade and dark brown skin. She was beautiful. Her brown plaid scarf was less for the Florida sun than for the cold that sometimes happens when you fly the friendly skies. Her black leggings and long-sleeved top were probably chosen for the same reason. Then there were the boots, of course. Her face was adorned by a gold nose ring and matching earrings that dangled and danced when she turned her head. Her dark hair, all but for the edges, hid under a brown hijab that contrasted with her scarf.

"Zone 1!" A voice blared over the PA.

As people passed by, she nervously touched her head. Her icy blue eyes darted around to see what others might have been on her. She played with the ends of her hijab and toyed with the idea of removing it. Her eyes fell on a man who stared at her unyieldingly. Slowly she turned away but glanced over her shoulder to see if he was still watching. He was. What was he thinking? Did her cinnamon complexion make her a threat? Was he wondering how *her* people could have eyes *that* color? Did she look "American enough"? She pulled the end of her hijab free and large, black curls fell upon her shoulders. At first the man still stared. But finally, he looked away. Nervously, she tucked her hair behind her ear and sipped her coffee. She looked defeated. My heart broke for her. I didn't know her destination. But I hoped it was one that was as beautiful as she was.

TK

PIECES

I admit it.

I'm broken.

I have spent all these years trying to look pretty

And polished for you but

It is senseless because I am the one who loses.

Your mind typically runs at one speed

While mine sprints randomly.

I have a hard time keeping pace

Yet I still added Pleasing You as more competition.

You have suggested that I find someone to talk to

When the one I want to talk to most is you.

You have robbed yourself of the

Majesty of me.

It is you who misunderstands

The world.

You see, the world is in the hands of people like me.

Every other day, we are standing out on the ledges

Of the universe.

We bravely feel the wind in our faces without

Knowing if it will burn us or chill us to the bone.

We humble ourselves and imagine a world without us.

We either feel deeply or not at all

But we usually feel out loud.

We have spoken to the flowers enough to know

How they feel when people like you ignore their beauty.

We have seen the world through enough tears

To know how beautiful it is when we have cloudless days.

We have found more of ourselves in heaps upon the floor

Than you have as you travel the globe.

It is true that I have always identified with broken things.

But now I make no apologies for being one of them.

I am fragmented and living freely.

Maybe someday, you will be worthy of all of my

Beautiful pieces.

TK

GRAVEYARD

Where does love go to die?

Maybe if I run fast enough, I can catch it before its last breath.

Then maybe for just a second, I can have

That beautiful dream I used to have and hold it in my hands

Even if only a moment.

For once, I won't have to try to recreate that feeling I had while I slumbered-

That feeling that for once, I am the only one who

Matters to someone—

Like maybe he isn't looking past me for the next girl who

Might be prettier, or taller, or thinner—

That feeling that there is actually hope for me and that I won't

Always be alone.

If I can find this amazing amorous apocalyptic place,

I can find a spark of that joy that has refused to die before I

Have a chance to see it.

Maybe if I run fast enough,

Love won't die before I do.

TK

HUNGER PAINS

I stockpiled some sugar overnight
But this morning, my supply is low.
Already, I need more from you.
I was just fed hours ago so
I shouldn't be so hungry.
But Baby, I'm ravenous.
I see you sleeping peacefully so
I am attempting to quiet the
Deep growls from within.
I could stare into the fridge for hours
But it has no remedy for this hunger.
I enjoy the dance you do in your sleep
And how the sheets trust the strength of your body
And are content to let you lead.
I fight the urge to ask to cut in.
I want you on my palate and my patience
Is growing thin.
At last, you awake.
You smile.
We feast.

TK

TOOLS OF WAR

This is not a pen and paper.
This is an arsenal.
It is what I take into war with me every day.
When no one else understands,
It is what identifies with me.
On the days anger and frustration take hold,
It is what gives me peace.
When I want to say words I will regret,
It is what helps me bite my tongue.
When I hurt from the bombs thrown at me,
It is what helps me blink back tears and keep fighting.
It helps me absorb the shocks of gut punches
This cold world throws my way.
When I am under attack,
It is my grenade.
When I am cut open and bleeding out,
It cleans and heals all wounds.
When I am the only soldier left on the field,
It multiplies and becomes a mighty and victorious battalion.
On the days I feel I won't make it home,
It is my map.
It is my weapon of choice.
I'm not sure what you're bringing into battle.
But I'm ready whenever you are.

TK

PEP TALK

Baby Girl, your lungs ain't broken.

You are just too smart to breathe in the bullshit.

They're mosquitoes.

They suck the life out of all that is beautiful.

But you, Firefly, just want to light up the world.

It's funny how in your corner of the world—

Where the colors sound loudest and the

Feelings taste sweetest, you inhale and exhale just fine.

You never have to worry about dark skies or dark nights

Because you make it all much brighter.

Just know that when you're feeling that weight

Sitting in the center of your chest, you are not broken.

Hold your breath and keep dreaming.

You are wise not to become what you behold.

TK

What do you say in your pep talk to yourself?

HEY, KALIEF

Hey, Kalief.

You don't know it. But you are my brother.

Seriously.

I have one at home just like you.

He's a gentle soul who can change the world.

But he so happens to have dark skin.

What he does or doesn't do never matters.

As long as he does or doesn't do it while

Wearing that dark skin,

There is no difference between his guilt and innocence.

At any given time, he can be beaten for wearing it.

He didn't go to solitary the way you did.

But he is isolated within the dirty walls of his trauma too.

He will always, in some way, be treated like that thing

That is adjacent to human.

He, too, finds himself trapped amongst groups

With which he doesn't belong.

Like you, he is accused of stealing something but

What they are saying he took are the things that should

Have been given to him anyway.

He should have had basic human decency handed to him on a platter

But again, because of the skin he wears, it is rationed.

He is allowed to exist but there is little respect for the space he occupies.

Those who feel they granted that space to him can come in

When they want and do what they want.

After all, they aren't the ones who wear the dark skin that

Seems to be a curse.

Kalief, I pray that unlike you, my brother never has a May 15, 2010.

With everything I have in me, I want to protect him.

But you see, I wear the dark skin too.

I am slightly more agile in mine because the aggression they assume

From me is not as strong as his.

When I don't smile, they might suspect anger.

But if he doesn't, he could end up in cuffs or worse.

I couldn't save you, Kalief.

For that I'm sorry.

And I know it sounds selfish to say that I don't want to

Cry the same tears your sister did.

But it would be a lie to say that wasn't my goal.

I failed you, Kalief.

But I am hoping and praying that I don't fail him too.

TK

ABOUT THE SKY

I love the sky.

I admire her quick sense of get-your-shit-togetherness

After a storm.

Within an instant, she can see past her troubles.

She wipes all the clouds from her face and

Dashes on some sunshine.

She doesn't hold in her anger either.

She lets her thunder roar loudly

So that we all know when something isn't right.

She uses her tears for whatever she wants.

She can either destroy or cultivate what is beneath her.

If she's feeling extra fancy,

She lays on some lightning and shows off a little.

If she just wants things to stand still for a while,

She shakes on some snow and stops them in their tracks.

She can bring about the worst

But when she bats her bright beautiful blues,

All is always forgiven.

She's bold.

She's powerful and she is wholly herself.

I want to be just like her.

TK

FREEDOM

To be able to give yourself to someone only when you choose—
And not those borrowed parts you had to sneak to pluck because you
Thought they looked pretty growing in your neighbor's yard
But now that they are planted in yours, they don't grow the same because your soil is different
No
I'm not talking about those parts at all
I'm talking about the parts of you that are innate
The parts that always grew within you organically
And never made room for the borrowed shit because it would just die there anyway
The parts you lived and thrived on from birth because they and you have always been enough
The parts of you that were healthy and vibrant because they were rested and whole
And not exhausted from searching for damns to give about everything
The parts of you that are content with celebrating yourself the way you see fit
And never being swayed by the thoughts of the parties you SHOULD be throwing
The parts of you that don't fear the tears but welcome them because
They nourish that good, organic, enough, healthy vibrant, content shit
You should be focused on anyway
To be able to decide NOT to give yourself to someone when you don't choose
To say "I'm keeping these parts for me"—
That's freedom.

TK

SAFETY

Come here, My Love.
The day is showing on your face.
When you're out there fighting,
Your armor is always expected to be strong
So, no one ever notices the cracks.
You have held it up for years so everyone assumes
The weight doesn't bother you.
But I can see it.
You're tired from having to fight against the gale force winds
That charge toward you.
Your stature is a bit misleading because you
Tower over much of the world but I know
That after being told for so long that you have no place in this world,
You only seek to disprove the theories.
Others don't know that you're breaking though.
To them, you are still intimidating,
That ominous thing that seeks to destroy what they have gained.
But I can see it.
All you want, even if just for a moment, is to be that version
Of you that everyone has forgotten.
You want to be surrounded by your favorite things,
To hurt without explanation
To laugh without suspicion
To cry without judgement
To love without fear.
To be protected.
Rest here.
You are safe with me.

TK

5 A.M.

Give yourself to me at 5 a.m.

I want those moments between dreams and coherence.

I want that second you open your eyes to greet the world.

I want the time before your mind forms

Its first thought of the day.

I want to be there when you start to happen.

At 5 a.m., you would keep nothing from me.

The tools you would need to do so

Will not have stretched their legs yet.

When you roll over and look at me,

I can watch your eyes adjust to my light

As you get to know me again.

When I touch you at 5 a.m.,

There is no time for engineered dirty thoughts to cross your mind.

At 5 a.m., you FEEL, purely and exclusively.

I have seen 5 a.m. many times over but now I know

That I want to see all of mine with you.

TK

I MADE YOU A MIXTAPE

I made you a mixtape of everything I have ever felt

And left it on your doorstep today.

I started with "The Day We Met" and the tune is kind of sweet.

It starts off slow and in certain places, it's cute and all over the place.

After that comes "That First Phone Conversation".

Be patient with that one because it's long and probing.

"Our First Date" comes next.

It's a song filled with questions but "I wonder if he wants to do this again as much as I do"

Is the best part.

"That Time We Took That Road Trip" and "When You Met My Friends" are

Happy, peppy tunes that will make your heart bounce a bit.

"The Day I Knew I Loved You" is deep and it lingers with every note.

It will start at your head and tell you everything glorious about yourself.

At the end, it fills the space so much that you will feel it stand next to you like flesh and blood.

"Pictures on The Wall" and "Waking Up to You"

Celebrate you even more and they may make you blush.

"Skin to Skin" will make the places you blush burn with pure passion.

"Late Hours at Work" and "No Time For Each Other" cool that off though.

"Growing Apart" is sad and will give you that feeling you get when you are falling

But rather than ever putting you out of your misery and

Letting you hit the ground,

It just repeats itself a few times.

"Why Don't You Love Me Anymore?" hurts because it is a song with no resolution.

The chords are unfinished and the melody changes constantly like it is frantic and

Has no clue what to do.

You can hear the death of us in the song but if you are anything like me,

You will keep listening and hoping you can fix it.

"What Does She Have That I Don't?" is awful because the lyrics will make you

Look at all the things that were once glorious

And find their defects.

"Saying Goodbye" is the worst because I am still not okay with the way that one sounds.

The notes, the lyrics, the cadence—everything about that one is off.

I left the mixtape for you.

You may just skip to the songs you like.

Then again, you may not listen at all.

In the end, you never did.

TK

If you could curate a soundtrack to your love life, what 10 songs would make the list? (Tip: You may want to write these in pencil.)

1. _____
2. _____
3. _____
4. _____
5. _____
6. _____
7. _____
8. _____
9. _____
10. _____

FOR REAL

When I fall in love—I mean fall in love for REAL—the feeling is going to need to be close to the one I get from music. When my heart is broken, I need to know that I don't hurt by myself. I need to laugh and sing to the tops of my lungs even when I don't know the words. I want to dance when I'm tired and nod my head to a beat created just for me. It needs to encourage me like The Staple Singers, tell my truth like PJ Morton, teach me like Donny Hathaway, speak to me like Miles Davis, move me like Floetry, understand me like John Legend, give me chills like Sam Cooke, make me a bit gutsy like Big K.R.I.T., put me together like Prince and show my greatness off like James Brown and Jill Scott. Yeah. When I fall in love—I mean fall in love for REAL—the melody is going to have to move through me. Otherwise, I'm just not doing it.

TK

PRICELESS

Are you expecting me to ask for the moon?

Are you dreading standing before a mighty merchant with

Only everything you have and feeling inadequate when you still can't afford it?

Do you dread seeing disappointment on my face

When I find out I will just have to watch it shine from a distance?

Are you thinking that pretty soon, I'll want

One of those pyramids I admire so much?

Do you think I will see you as less of a man when you tell me

I will just have to be content seeing them between pages?

Do you think I'll ask for the world?

Do you think I'll think you don't love me when you tell me

You came up short and couldn't haggle for me?

You really do have it all wrong.

All I want is that honesty your face used to carry

When you said you loved me.

I want the heaviness of your mind and that feather light feeling

Of hearing you laugh.

I want that peaceful babbling just before you fall asleep.

I want the gentle rise and fall of your chest as you dream.

I want the sweetness of your celebrations and the

Stark bitterness of the lessons you learn.

It is not humanly possible to put a price on those.

You are the most valuable currency I know.

TK

PAUL REVERE

Fuck you and the horse your rode in on.
You decided to breeze through my life and
Wreck everything in the process.
I carried a torch for you and I trusted you to hold the flame
But I never thought you would use it to burn me.
It's easy at this point for you to ride by when you see me breaking
Because you never got off that horse in the first place.
Sure, you would bend down to kiss me
And hoist me up to defile me.
But you never brought yourself down to common ground
With me.
When I said, "I love you", it must have sounded different by the
Time it reached you up there.
They sounded like divine words to me because you said
It back from such an altitude.
When I said I missed you, it was easy for you
Because you could look down from where you were and
Catch a glimpse of me
So, you never missed me at all.
You're okay with the fire you set and all the fortresses
You have leveled within me
Because, after all, you have that damn horse.
So, keep riding.
Pretend to care and leave behind your crocodile tears.
As you ride off into the sunset,
I will pretend I would be sad if that same sun
Burns you along your way.

TK

WHAT HAPPENED TO SANDRA BLAND?

What are you trying to tell me? Your eyes keep haunting me as though you really do want me to know what happened to you. Unfortunately, you can't part your lips. Are you wanting me to know that they took you from us and treated you like some marionette that they dressed, posed and pulled strings on so that you told the story they saw fit? The fact that the keen, sculpted point you had to your nose is completely gone, your skin that was once a lot like mine now shows ominous blotches and your crown and glory falls backwards as though caught in the wind tells me something isn't right. As you lie upon that floor knowing that your regal frame of 6 feet did not perish from only 5, your spirit practically screams "Foul play!" I know firsthand that depression can be fought with life and I know you knew that too. It's true. You had your flaws. We all do. You knew so much about our people's struggles so I had hopes that soon you would be able to see the light on the struggles of ALL of us. Because you also knew your rights and fought for them, you had to be the example. Dear martyr, the heads of the guilty hit their pillows but tears of sorrow hit mine. Strong-willed and opinionated, I know you would tell me what happened if you could. But now you never will.

TK

GRAND CANYON

I can't close the chasm.
Instead, the only thing I can do is stare at you across this great divide.
I can see you self-destructing from where I'm sitting.
You aren't recovering from your injuries very well.
You are mistaken to think that just because you
Can't see my scars that I no longer have any.
It was a long time ago that I clawed my way out of the trench
But some wounds just don't heal.
My love legs are still fractured but all these years,
I have been able to tone down my limp.
So, instead of thinking I'm hurting,
You think I'm just being cool about it.
It's not that "cool" that keeps me from mentioning it.
The truth is, I'm hoarse from screaming at you
In a language you don't understand anymore.
I don't even have the peace of a babbling stream below
To count on.
Instead, I pass the time watching the migrations of
Buzzards overhead that wait to eat your dead things as soon as you let them go.
But you hold on to your dead things.
You hold them much tighter than you ever held me.
You hold them because they are familiar.
When you need a reason to blame someone else,
They provide.
They keep you empty and allow you to fill yourself
With the things that will keep you wanting.
Your wanting makes you feel alive.
It gives you purpose.
While you grip your dead things, your eyes are fixed on me.
Since I can't speak to you,
I try to send you pieces of my heart.
But even they don't reach anymore.
They get about halfway to you then they run out of steam
And fall to their deaths.
Rather than run out of pieces to send you,
I stay still and hope your curiosity about the pieces you've missed
Will get the best of you.

I hope you will let go of those things that will never again have a pulse
And climb down to look for them.
I hope that this fissure, this break,
This gaping hole we love across
Can someday make a wonder of itself.

TK

ON WRITING

I like to stand on the edge of myself when I write. I like to step outside and stare back at every emotion I could ever imagine. It is the only time I can look at all of me at once. It is that standing naked in front of the ultimate mirror of truth that frees me. When I look at my fears, I don't always have to look for the ways to overcome them. In those moments, I really don't have to be heroic. I can hurt and never have to explain why. I can cry without the embarrassment of anyone seeing my face when I do it. I can be angry. I can yell on the page and still get a second chance to rationally approach a situation. When I am writing, I can just be. It seems like when I am writing, I always seem to fall in love the right way. If it's mutual, I grow. If not, I learn. When I'm writing, that special person always touches me just the way I need them to and they always allow me to touch them the way that every part of me desires. I am never left wanting. I get to love without complication. And so, I write.

TK

SHAMIKA

God dedicated The Moon to you that night.
He must have because we had never seen it that way before.
He gave it a new red dress to wear once it took off
The black one it wore to that party a few years back.
It got all fancy for us.
He must have known it was the last time I would see you.
He knew it was the last time you would smile at me
And the last time I would hear your voice.
You and I had to see The Moon put on her new dress
Before you left.
You didn't have much energy for dancing but
She knew that She still had to get dressed for you.
You're special, My Love.
You always have been.
You couldn't stay for the party and
I was a bit too sad to dance without you.
But it is good to know that you made it to the other party that
God threw in your honor.
You did get a chance to rest on your journey to meet Him.
He healed your pain along the way and took away all your worry.
When you arrived, He had your dancing shoes laid out for you
And a dress much brighter than the one He had given The Moon.
Now you have energy to dance for days.
And Aunt Elaine has been waiting to show you some joyous moves.
The Moon and her dress are no match for you.
God dedicated the moon to you that night.
He knew that you and She were majesty like none had ever seen.

TK

(January 20, 2019. The night of the Super Wolf Blood Moon and our last time together on Earth.)

PRINCESS NOBODY

I should have known I couldn't be Cinderella.

They don't make glass slippers big enough for these feet.

Just like the rest of me, they are too big,

Too much and all over the place.

These hands aren't made for rings.

Bright symbols of love just don't belong here.

There are far too many dreams in this head for a crown to fit.

And I don't have a face that says any of them will come true.

I'm not Snow White either-

Even if any fruit I am given does have the intention to poison me.

Yes, someday my prince will come.

But he will wave to me, thank me for clearing his path

And ride on to meet the fairest in the land.

Like Belle, I have found my beast,

But it isn't me that he is looking to transform for.

He is looking for the rose with the enchanted petals,

Not the one with the noticeable thorns.

So, I will stay here, high up in this tower,

Longing for the happy ending not meant for me.

TK

GOOD RIDDANCE

Girl, thank you for taking him off my hands!

Now he can be *your* sorry excuse for a man.

Honestly, he's useless.

It took me this long to see.

But I'm sure he told you he was God's gift to me.

Well, he didn't come in a pretty package.

He wasn't tied with a bow.

He left me patting my pockets and asking,

"Where'd that gift receipt go?"

I wanted to return him.

A prize, he is not.

He was already in the cart but thanks for meeting me in the parking lot.

I was looking for a man who was ready, willing and able.

But instead, I took home petty, weak and emotionally unstable.

Maybe you will be the girl he brags on and always flaunts.

But I hope he doesn't switch gears on you the moment you don't

Do what he wants.

If you pick him up when he is down and help him better himself,

I hope he isn't using your light to help him love someone else.

When you call him out for being radio silent for days at a time,

I hope he doesn't look at you like you have lost your mind.

When all you have ever wanted was to build a family,

I hope he doesn't avoid the subject the way he did with me.

When you just want to spend every night with him,

I hope you don't end up wondering just where the hell he's been.

My shackles are off.

I'm free!

This is the end of my sentence.

You may say "He's mine now".

But Sweetie, I just say "Good riddance".

TK

BUILD

I want that "I've never seen it. But I hear it's beautiful"
Kind of relationship with you.
No, really. Those are the conversations I want to have.
I want us to talk about all the things we have been told
Were wondrous and dream of seeing them together.
I'm talking about the rain in Spain,
The peaks of the pyramids and the lights of The Eiffel Tower.
But after we make that list,
I want us to take those steps to creating a future.
I want us to be able to forget about all the old things
That didn't allow us to witness wonders.
I want to not even be able to see the
Old shanties of shame for all the new
Pitched roofs of positivity we have put up.
I want us both to know that not living in nirvana now
Doesn't mean we can never make it.
We have all the materials we need.
So, let's just build our Beautiful.

TK

SECRET OF THE SUN

The sun told me a secret today.

She finally admitted that there actually is

Something special she does when she shines on you.

She does this thing where she reaches inside

Of you and pulls everything I love to the surface.

She brings the things I'm learning

To love too.

She positions them at different angles

And lets me see them in all new light.

She never admitted it before

Because she wasn't sure how I would feel

About her doing something different

When she shines on me.

But right now,

I'm looking at all of you in the light.

And I'm not mad at all.

TK

STARING AT STAFF PAPER

I can only hope to someday be as important as a single note of music. It carries the beauty of being a part of an arrangement or being everything and nothing on its own. It meets with friends to build movements to propel life forward or stands alone and repeats itself and causes life to stand still. It is lonely, but it is also the best company kept. A single music note understands that when you don't belong anywhere, you can thrive everywhere. When she is sad, she is beautiful. When she is happy, she is radiant. When she stands alone, she is strong. When she is vulnerable, it is accepted and the undying support makes her strong again. She is imperfect. She is everything.

TK

LOST ONE

I am Success's displaced child.

I know the comfort of her embrace because

I was born to be hers.

But our home is war torn.

Over the years, bombs have flown and

Fires of failure and fear have separated us.

The debris of doubt blocks our path.

But I will keep crying out.

A mother never forgets her child's voice.

I will keep fighting.

I will find my way home to her.

TK

CHANGED

It's too late.
We've loved and now we can't turn back.
We will never again be those same
People we used to be.
Suddenly, we're so deep that we fall
Into ourselves sometimes.
We can formulate thoughts but they
Get wrapped around emotions and
Sometimes don't make it out.
We have never known the
Joyful fear we are about to enter into
Because there is only one place it exists.
We entered the realm when our hearts
Were opened and the portal sealed up behind us.
I'm sure there is a science to learning
To live differently.
We now have to add watching and trusting
To our behavior.
We have become lovers.
And never again can we be anything else.

TK

SIGNS

Something in the wind says we're not going to make it.

Maybe it's the way it blew eerily over me this morning

And made me think of jackets

Rather than having your arms to hold me close.

The sun came in on the conversation and was sweet enough to

Replace the wind but made me think of being in

A barren desert

Rather than the many articles of clothing I could remove before

Getting next to you.

I think the trees know something too because they don't sway freely

In the breeze but teeter rapidly in indecision.

The clouds are aware, I know, because they float away from me

As if to flee to someone with better luck.

The grass can't fool me either.

I know it has intentionally become less bountiful beneath my feet

And left me with only a hard ground to contend with.

Water, doesn't flow the same way.

Its ripples make not exclamation points but

Sad eyes that apologize with every blink.

Hills no longer rise to meet me but wave farewell at a distance.

Rainbows don't say hello but tuck their heads behind the clouds.

The babbling brook says nothing but leaves an uncomfortable silence.

Raindrops frantically fall on my face to hide all traces of tears.

The lightning and the thunder cease because they pity me.

You and I aren't meant to be.

And the entire world knows it.

TK

TRANSPLANT

Let's trade hearts for a second.

Since you seem so convinced that this one will heal,

Everything should be fine, right?

You keep telling me it won't always be broken,

So, the pain you inherit should be temporary.

I've already done the hard part and

And bore the fresh breaks and bleeding.

The only thing you have to do is

Hold still so the pieces don't go where they shouldn't.

You tell me everything will be fine

But I feel like it's the end.

So, if I put my broken heart with your brain that knows everything,

It should all work out.

Right?

If I'm as great as you say I am,

I deserve to be as lighthearted and carefree as you.

Don't I?

I appreciate your sympathy

But what I would really appreciate

Is if you would take over for a while.

If you believe what you say,

It should all be over soon.

TK

RUNNING IN PLACE

You change me.

You make me second guess everything I say and do.

You always make me feel like I am just not SOMETHING enough.

With all the gusto of a foolish schoolgirl,

I have the nerve to pursue you.

You're broken and emotionally unavailable

And the truth is, I would die before the pursuit is a success.

I am in awe of you.

So, I fool myself into thinking that the

Breadcrumb trail of communication you grant me is enough.

Deep down, I know that with you,

I will always be starving.

I will want what you refuse to give as a result of your own

Arrogance and knowing that you are

What I want most.

There will always be that looming feeling

Of inferiority and fatigue of just

Trying to be SOMETHING enough.

But I must keep running.

I have to outrun my desire for you.

That is, if I ever want to save myself.

TK

WHOAMAN

I have decided that it is time for my revolution.

Here and now,

I'm raising a fist and my voice.

Long silenced by the so-called strength of my counterpart,

I am just about ready to belt out a tune.

Man is called strong while it is I who

Bear the children,

Birth and nurse the children,

Manage the home,

Work harder for less pay and

Navigate emotions about the crumbling world alone

All while putting myself AND my man back together.

Several times, I have been a tree that has fallen in the forest.

But because I feared it waking my children,

I couldn't afford to make a sound.

But enough of that.

I'm slinging my baby onto my hip, taking my briefcase in hand

And creating my own damn forest.

The soil will be rich with my hope and perseverance and

The roots to all my fellow trees will have undying support.

There, we will all stand

Strong

Proud

Unmoving

And more majestic than any man could ever dream.

TK

INVESTED

You're my new wallet. You are that precious thing I have been given that I am keeping someplace safe. Though I know you're there, every now and then, I check to be sure. If I haven't seen you in a while or you aren't in my line of sight, I begin to retrace my steps. I wonder if I have truly lost you and what I could have done to prevent it. But when you come back, I light up. I am aware that there is a chance you won't be around forever, but I wish for it anyway. You see, shortly after I got you, I placed my remaining hope for love within you. I gave you my last $5. So, in addition to thinking you're nice to look at, I'm invested in you. Rather than have you leave and allow my heart to suffer the pains of bankruptcy, I subconsciously check the pocket nearest to my heart to be sure you are still there. You're my new wallet—the most beautiful thing I have seen in quite some time.

TK

BLACK MAN

I remember you.

I'm not talking about this thuggish version of you that

They want everyone to believe.

I only know your royalty.

I see how you protect the Black Woman and lead your kingdom.

I see how, despite everything, you always keep pushing through.

When you're in danger, the sirens don't sound for you.

But you persist through the fear.

When they say you're not fit to learn,

You rise and teach the masses.

They never expect you to take care of your children,

But you nurture and raise them as kings and queens.

I see the way you love others even at the times

You struggle to love yourself.

I appreciate you.

TK

NOT ANYMORE

I used to wish that love would come to find you.

Even though you and I didn't work,

I wanted to believe that deep down you were still good and kind.

I wanted to believe that we would both get our happy ending

Even if we weren't together.

Life pulled no punches when it came to teach you lessons.

Some of which you have grown from,

Others, you are still striving to screw up perfectly.

So much about you has changed

But I still see glimmers of the old you.

I have learned a lot.

I no longer wish for love to come find you.

But now I offer it my apologies.

Now I know that love deserves much better than you.

TK

BROKEN LINES

I have no clue how to express myself

But I do it anyway.

Instead of "I really like you",

It comes out as the constant "WYD" that probably has you rolling your eyes.

Instead of "Would you like to go out?",

It comes out, "We should hang out sometime".

"Hang out"? Are we thirteen?

Rather than "I miss you" or "I want to see you",

I say, "If you are ever in the area…"

I don't just say "I love you".

I give you some goofy ass "I think you're cool."

I don't even say "I was thinking about you".

You just get a lame "Hey".

And I know you are worth so much more.

I understand you are confused about how I feel.

What's worse is that I know exactly how I feel

But I am holding back.

Who am I saving it for? No one else is worthy.

If I would just grow up a little before I address you,

I can stop doing you these disservices.

Maybe if I just leave you alone and start my growing now,

I may be worthy of you by the time

You even notice that I am missing.

TK

NOTHING COMPARES 2 U

Damn the Mona Lisa.
The Sistine Chapel is a bore.
All the painted things think they are art
Because they've never seen you before.
You're not confined to clay or stuck up on a wall.
You see life.
You see beauty.
You move through us all.
You make Picasso jealous.
Romare Bearden? Who is he?
If anyone wants to see real art,
I'll just show them you, honestly.
I'll show them how you sigh and lay your head upon my chest.
The way you say my name is perfection, nothing less.
I'll show them the way you glance at me
And smile between your words.
I'm sure they'd agree your voice is
The sweetest sound ever heard.
You're much more hypnotizing than Dali.
You pose.
You talk.
You dance.
Nothing else in the history books will ever stand a chance.
MoMa, The Louvre, Uffizi—
They can tour them all if they want to.
They can ooh and ahh until they're tired.
But nothing compares to you.

TK

NO LOVE

I ain't writing about love today.

I don't care how much you want to hear about butterflies

And somebody making you weak in the knees.

You won't get it from me today.

I don't have time to plant flowers

In the barren field that you call your imagination.

Don't expect me to give you the words to say

To the one you feel you can't do without.

If you want an eargasm or that warm feeling in

Your literary loins,

You are out of luck.

You will have to look elsewhere for that poetic pitter patter

And the sonnets that set your soul ablaze.

Talk to somebody else about love.

'Cause today,

It just ain't on my mind.

TK

COME CLOSER

Come a little closer

And let me taste your soul.

Let me lick along the lines of

Your intellect and taste what nourishment it yields.

Allow me to caress your pride

Until it stands at attention.

Give me permission to massage your mind

And if only for a moment,

Mold it to fit me perfectly.

Grant me passage to knead your tenderness

So that it merges well with my own.

Say it's okay that I gently kiss your grace

So that it never wants to leave.

Say I can nibble on your imagination

And make it sing a happy tune.

Come closer.

Let me experience you.

TK

UNPACKING

Yeah, I've been MIA these past few days.

That's because I have been busy unpacking.

I have a lot of things to sort out in my heart and head

Before I can allow myself leisurely time again.

There are far too many boxes marked

"Triggers" and "Unresolved Issues" blocking my way

For me to go out and have a good time.

You and I have been doing that

"Maybe it'll take your mind off of it"

Thing for too long.

That's why I'm blocked in this corner now.

All of the boxes filled with

Depression, anxiety, fear and hurt feelings

Have left me with only a corner of myself to live in.

And I'm a house with an open floor plan.

So, you KNOW that's all wrong.

Right now, I can't even see down my own hallway,

Let alone see how to let you in.

Just give me a little more time to

Unpack and get things in order.

I'll see you again soon.

TK

LOVE

I write about you all the time. Those who don't know any better would think I knew you personally. Like a child holding on to some pipe dream of her favorite celebrity, I write scripts in my head of what I will say the day we meet. I dream that you will say you love my work and that someday we should collaborate. I watch as you move through the crowd sharing laughs and hugs with everyone you are more familiar with. My heart pounds as your fragrance fills the air. How I wish that just once, I could be the one on your arm. But here I am, writing scripts that will never play out. And you, my precious star, remain a dream far beyond my reach.

TK

HAPPILY, NEVER AFTER

Dear Cinderella,

There just aren't enough happy endings to go around. Some of our carriages really are just pumpkins and our fairy godmothers are just regular people with generous listening ears. No matter how much they love us, they will never have wands and they can never grant out hearts' desires. The regular rags we wear are all that remain when we look in the mirror. There will be no gowns or grand balls for us to attend. We don't get princes and our slippers are not made of glass. We have more than two wicked stepsisters and we are constantly on guard. At the end of our suffering, we don't get to live in castles. Nothing eases the pain or the memories of the loved ones we have lost. When we open our windows, we don't plan for the birds to know all the words to our songs. Nine times out of ten, they are just ditties we made up to get us through the day. We can sweep all we want, but everything is still dirty. We get nowhere. But we work so that we have purpose. We tell ourselves it will pay off. Watching you live and fall in love as you see the shiniest treasures of life allow those of us who weren't born to be princesses to have a glimmer of hope. At night, we tuck ourselves in with your tales and just hope they fill our dreams. We want to be convinced that we are worthy, if only for a moment.

Sincerely,

The Other Half

TK

BE ART

Give me goosebumps.

Make me tremble like the feel of a cool breeze over me.

Lie with me and watch my face light up when

Stevie sings.

Give me a joyous shout loud enough to match my own when I

Hear Prince growl.

Fly with me when I read Zora's words and

Follow the furl in my brow when

Maya speaks to me.

When Jean-Michel amazes me,

Return the air to my lungs.

Come with me when Carrie Mae and Gordon's pictures

Move me.

Sit next to me when I learn

From Spike, Lena and Ava.

Join in on the grit and grime from Coogler.

Even if you aren't a poet,

Lay pretty and honest words on my ears

But don't be afraid to let the ugly truth slip through.

When I am all over the place,

Love the place I am all over.

Behold the artist in me.

Love me when I create.

Get inspired by me.

TK

Note: This is not my view of all men of the cloth. But those to which it applies, you know who you are.

AFTER CHURCH

Pastor, can I talk to you for a moment?
Your sermon got the saints fired up today.
You really did your job.
But on behalf of us who actually believe we are
Imperfect, I have a few questions.
You got a big response when you talked
About how young girls today need to prepare
Themselves to be the wives of tomorrow.
But Pastor, when will our husbands
Start their training?
When will the classes on cherishing your
Woman be taught?
And are we just gonna act like Sister Johnson
And Sister Williams don't have sons who
Have no clue they are brothers because
We're preserving Deacon Lawrence's name?
Wouldn't these young men or,
"Husbands of tomorrow" if you will,
Benefit from the example of a man who
Owned up to his transgressions?
And since many other future husbands
Are within earshot,
Shouldn't Deacon Evans stop eyeballing
Tiffany when she walks by and commenting
On how she's "built like a woman"?
I mean, she's only eleven.
From you, we always hear
"Seek and ye shall find".
So why is it frowned upon when I seek
Understanding by studying the Qur'an
In addition to my Bible?
I mean, essentially they
Say the same things.
Is it really so bad that I would rather research
Than always take your word and keep
Staring at that picture of Kenny Loggins
In a robe before I bow my head in prayer?
His skin just doesn't look like bronzed clay to me.
That's all I'm saying.
But you, Sir, had plenty to say when LaShawn
Came to church with last night's club stamp

On her hand.
But no one said anything when
You stood in the pulpit with Sister Allen's
Lipstick on your collar.
Maybe I was the only one who saw that though.
You have had a long day, I know.
You probably want to go home and unwind,
Maybe throw back a few beers the way
You did during the incoherent phone calls
You made to me while I was away in college.
I appreciate you calling to check on me.
I just wish I could have understood you.
You said it was the devil's elixir for a reason.
I know you have to leave.
Speaking of which, that's a nice
New car you've got there.
It's good to see they are paying you well.
It must be because you take such good
Care of the Building Fund.
I'm just waiting to see the building you
MUST be building for us elsewhere.
It has to be spectacular because we have
Been contributing since I was ten and
This roof still leaks.
And I never found that verse in the Bible
That says all of my tattoos are bigger
Sins than your daughter's collection of
Baby daddies.
I'm sure it's in there because you imply it all the time.
But can you point it out?
And I'm sure you know where it says
That my mama's divorce is less holy
Than an eternity in a loveless marriage too.
Can you also show me where God said it was okay
For you and Sister Allen to be together because her marriage
Is "technically over"?
You don't have to show me now.
We can talk about it later since I know
You need to get to the track before they stop taking bets.
I had better take off this jacket before I
Go outside though.

I need to be prepared for all the
Fire and brimstone you'll send my way.
Have a good day, Pastor.
See you next Sunday.

TK

NOT THE GIRL

I'm not the girl you fight for.

I'm not the one you regret losing and spend your whole

Life trying to get back.

I am not the girl who is responsible for the lonely tears

You cry at night.

I am not the girl who years after loving and losing me,

You just hope that another can measure up to.

I am the girl who loves faithfully and in spite of.

I am the girl who forgives and accepts apologies that have never

Actually been given.

I am the girl who wants to build a life with the one she loves.

I am that girl who speaks life into all you do.

I am the girl who wants to love you and only you

And do so perfectly.

I am that girl who knows the meaning of the word unconditionally.

I am not the girl you fight for because,

If you're smart, I'm the girl you should never want to lose in the first place.

TK

THE SORRY YOU DIDN'T SAY

I forgive you for loving me the way fools do.

You probably don't regret not seeing me just yet.

But I trust that someday you will.

You will think about the times I poured my heart out to you

And you never even bothered to follow the tide.

You will think about the times I said your name

And you couldn't hear the music in my voice.

You will think about the times I wrapped my arms around you

But you still turned cold.

You will pray for a random call from me in the middle of the day.

You will wish that you had given me everything.

You will look at all the wasted years

And calculate all the investments you should have made in us.

Their returns will astound you.

The days and nights when you are at your loneliest,

You will miss me.

But for now, I will just know that you're sorry

Or that if you aren't, you will be.

I give you my forgiveness.

And I give my aching heart its due rest.

TK

'ROUND MIDNIGHT

Usually 'round midnight,

I think of you.

Right in the center of my brain,

I build your universe.

I smirk at Fate

Because I am in on the secret.

I already know the joys

Of Me and My Thoughts

Being alone together.

TK

ASHES TO ASHES: THE CASE FOR CREMATION

When it is time for me to leave,
Please let me go.
Don't bury me in a vault in preparation
For visitors I cannot receive.
Do not make me and my shortcomings
Fertilizer for the food that nourishes
The lives of others.
I don't want them to bear the aftertaste
Of my failures.
I don't want my doubts planted
In their souls.
I won't be sad that you have released me.
It will be my greatest joy.
I want you to let me fly in the wind.
My heart won't break because no one
Loves me.
For then, there will be hope of landing
Upon the cheek of someone who has
Known love.
I will mix with their tears of joy and
Finally know the taste.
I won't cry for the children I don't have.
Maybe then I can linger upon nursery
Windows and hear the gleeful
Little laughs I missed.
I won't think twice about how I have
Disappointed my friends and family.
Then I can wrap 'round roots of trees
And they can FINALLY see me grow.
I won't hurt for the beauty I don't have.
Then, I will be a part of the
Growing grass
The blowing wind
The rolling seas

The majestic thunder
The piercing lighting
The ever-present sky.
Do not cry for me.
Do not sit with a shell of me.
Do not let me stop your lives
When mine is done.
Instead, place me on the wind
And just let me go.

TK

SENTIMENTAL MOOD

Sometimes the rain

Makes me feel sentimental.

But most of the time,

It just makes me feel…you.

TK

ZORA

There is something in your gaze for me. There is a certain beauty to that cockiness in your smirk. It's a lesson in the power of always knowing something they don't. When I was ten, I learned your name. When I read your words, I looked around and no one understood you the way I did. I knew we were kindred spirits. Though I never saw the bony mule, there, I would find the best stories. You showed me how to hunt a story like a lioness, quiet and steady with a ferocious final pounce. When you told stories on the porch, I felt those experiences in my soul. I sat by you in The Sassy Susie as you tore down the streets. Through you, I saw the beauty in our people. When we laugh our big laughs and play the dozens, it is then that we sit closest to God. We use "ain't" and "y'all" even when we know better. And it is glorious. You were a Finer Woman long before I was born and long before I ever knew I wanted to be. But I had already taken your advice and started sharpening my oyster knife. You did it. So, I knew it was a good idea. I wanted to speak like you, walk like you and write like you. You were my guru. Hats tipped, long skirts, pants with high waists—you were equal parts grit and grace. Coming in with SPUUUUUUUUUUUUUNNNNNK and making sure everyone paid attention, you were all I needed to be. I say "needed" because you were the type of woman it would take decades for me to grow into. I watched my mother and grandmother closely the same way you did because I knew I would find a lot of my fodder there. Sometimes I wonder if you met my mother and whispered to her on that fall day that I was conceived. It seems you told her that on the day of the birth of Baldwin, she would bring forth a daughter who aspired to his uprightness and your tenacity and that the world would not be prepared. Like you, I didn't have a place, so I would have to make my own. I feel you every time I pick up a pen. I can see that smirk of yours when the thoughts start flowing. I want to write things that you would want to read. I want to pick up where you left of and tell the ugliest, most beautiful stories of us. I can only hope I make you proud.

TK

FORGET ME LOTS

Every day I have unwrapped your neglect.

I wish I could feign surprise at this point.

Your ribbons of rejection lay all around me

And there is nothing pretty about them.

Your bows of bypass perch all around me like shadows.

When you happen to remember me,

I do my best to muster up a note of excitement.

"Aw, you shouldn't have!"

Except, I mean you… really…. shouldn't have.

It would be more gracious of you to

Just ignore me all the time.

Then at least we won't have to pretend it is some

Grand gala when you make your presence known.

Just a thought.

TK

BE FREE

I've never sought to cage a bird
That begged to be set free.
I respect its desires to be anywhere
Other than here with me.
Whether that bird be a lover
Or a once trusted friend,
I take heed to the fact that
Sometimes forever ends.
That bird should not be angry when I
Watch it fly away from me.
For I am doing as it has asked
And letting it be free.

TK

THE BEAUTIFUL STRUGGLE

"My art hurts." That's all I can say on days like this. These are the days when it hurts to create. I search for happy thoughts to write down. But I'm no fool. I don't believe a single one of them. I only attempt to close the door because I don't want my demons to get out. When they run rampant, they become difficult to wrangle and will destroy everything in their paths. And I would never wish that upon anyone. But for as much effort as I put up to control those feelings of sadness, fear and doubt, they bang loudly upon everything I am. When they knock, I use the sound to measure just how far I am from where I want to be. It's deafening. Rather than waste words, I usually just cry on paper. When I say it all out loud, it always seems to come out in another language and no one understands. When I speak, people give answers where there are no questions and ask questions for which there are no answers. So, I sit and write. I let my pain run free and I do not treat its rabidity. It grabs hold of my passion, gnashes its teeth and engages in battle. Pain and Passion toss and tussle their way around my self-doubt. They fight and well up inside of me and I attempt to write out the hurt. I get cut, bruised and I bleed a lot. But I am lucky enough to always find beauty in the struggle.

TK

FUNCTIONAL

For you, I am Van Gogh's ear.

By that, I mean I may not be your entire story,

But I am the part that makes you intriguing.

While I may not be that one thing that makes you famous,

A lack of me would leave your story wanting.

You have had decades of eternities—

Things that drew themselves out

Seemingly just to spite you.

But the look in your eyes tells me that your forever—

That thing that never lasted but you wanted it to—

Didn't come before you kissed me.

I am all of your vices—

Those things that inflame you and give you purpose

But make you the least attractive to others.

I am that thing you can choose to live without

But my absence makes you the most imbalanced.

Like Frida's brow, I lead you from vision to vision.

My guidance, though bold and harsh,

Serves its purpose and enhances your beauty.

Regardless of ear or eyebrow,

I remain that one piece about the masterpiece

Of life that you so foolishly ignore.

TK

UP

Where are you right now?

Where is your mind?

These stars tell me your mind is on me.

But they probably lie.

All pretty things do.

We're written in them.

And because they loom over me as I sleep,

They're at the best angle to fill my head with happy things-

A kiss

A laugh

A touch

A life.

I don't know if these stars are lying or

Whether or not what we have is real.

But for now, I'll just stay here,

Blissfully looking up.

TK

BLACK PEOPLE

I love the way we love each other.

The silence and mere nodding of heads as

We pass on the street says so much.

The prolonged games of Spades in the backyard

With the grill going

Frankie Beverly & Maze blasting

The chants of "Who made this?!"

Echoing through the kitchen

Nicknames like Canopy, Lil' Rich, Lil' Buddy

Dank, Popcorn, Goo-Goo and Peanut

That stick so well we forget given names

Learning to drive on Daddy's lap on long dirt roads

At the age of 6

Hardly putting on a pair of shoes for an entire summer

Sitting for hours and enduring the gripping of braids

That hurt a little for a moment but make our crowns more glorious

In the long run

Obligatory rounds of The Electric Slide at functions

And involuntary folding of the lips and wagging of the tongues

Complete with body rolls when our jam comes on

Skin ashy when fresh out of the tub

But shining like black gold after a touch of cocoa butter

Skin smooth, dark and usually looking

At least ten years younger than our chronological age

The way we walk and talk

The way we say "Nigga" knowing that we probably shouldn't

But feeling empowered when it comes from those who love us

Well-seasoned chicken

Hairstyles that defy gravity

Roots responsible for the birth of civilization

Grandmama's living room filled with cousins and play cousins

And a whole lot of love

Thick bottomed girls who grow more beautiful the more

They understand their ample assets

Men who carry themselves like royalty without a day of instruction

While holding the potential to do everything

The resilience to withstand a clutching of a purse when we enter elevators

Our faces being pressed against the hot hoods of police cars

And the intimidation we cause when we travel in groups

The power to show what we have created from hundreds of years of slavery

And using that same power to walk into any room knowing that our ancestors

Are responsible for the creation of someone, something and possibly

Everything in it

The way we say "Boo", "Baby" or "Suga" and make everyone want to

Emulate us

How we call a fellow melanite we have never met "Bro" or "Sis"

And it instantly feels like a family reunion

The way we are everywhere,

Everything

And we are always the vein—

I love that.

TK

THE OTHER WOMAN

I've been asked if I hated her. Honestly, for a while, I did. But you know how they say hate is a wasted emotion? When I stopped hating her, I knew that to be true. I had allowed that hate for her to fill my head and heart so much that I no longer knew how to use all of me to prosper. I realized we were both dumb. We both believed his pretty words. But I pity her more than me. I knew him before he became that thing he couldn't recognize when he looked in the mirror. She touched his body when he belonged to someone else. I held his heart when it belonged only to me. I knew him in his purity when art and love fueled him. I knew him before he wore the mask of shame over his face. He wants to be in my life again because when you're unforgettable, they always come back. The Other Woman and I simply don't move in the same circles. We don't vibrate on the same frequency. Because of that, hating her really would be a waste. I learned from my pain. Her being The Other Woman and being left to hurt, grow and heal on my own is what showed me how utterly amazing I am.

TK

MS. CELLOPHANE

I've gotten really good at watching other
People fall in love.
I've gotten not looking jealous when I see that
Glimmer in their eyes down to a science.
I am so good at pretending I don't feel like my empty arms
Are useless when I see them hold each other.
I curl my lips into a smile each time I
See them kiss.
When I hear them say "I love you",
I pretend there's someone at home waiting to
Say it to me.
When they dance, I pretend I have never
Heard the song that plays
And I hang on every note until the end.
When I see them in pictures,
I focus on how green the grass looked
The day it was taken
Or I pretend to care where the people in the
Background are going.
When they exchange vows,
I pretend someday someone will say
Even prettier things to me.
The lovers watch me watch them.
I do it so well
That they never know that I'm there.

TK

DON'T GIVE UP

Do you ever have those times in life when you are doing all you can and it seems nothing works? Well, My Dear, that is because you are not doing all you can. I say that not placing blame but letting you know from experience that those moments are designed to teach you that you are destined for greatness beyond your wildest dreams. There will be challenges and there will be tears. But know that it is okay to break so that you can build. I, for one, am already proud of you and cannot wait to see what you become. So, I beg of you, please don't give up.

TK

LIQUIDITY

I love the way you flow through me.

Your voice is like hot lava through my mind.

Your words set fires with each syllable.

When you touch me, each finger is a ribbon of

Hot butter over my soul.

You drench me.

Your gaze covers me like hot wax and makes me

A cocoon of myself.

You make me see me.

You are the river that drowns me.

My lungs are full of you.

But you are that nectar that I thirst for.

You leave me wanting more.

Your strength carries me to great distances

Some of which I never knew existed.

Though I never know where I might end up,

I surrender and float away in you.

TK

LITTLE ONE

I want you to have it all. I want you well-fed. I want your soul to never know that feeling of being hungry. I want you to never feel the need to be put into a box to feel closeness. I want all of you to run free. You will cry. But I want none of those tears to be because you feel I have left you. I am always open to you. I have no exact picture of what I want you to be. Even if I did, you would be too large to fit into it. I could never draw lines strong enough to hold your colors. Any frame I could craft would crack and splinter under the weight of your imagination. You are never wrong for your emotions but when they make you feel lost, I will help you chart the course. I am proud of you even in all the nothingness you do. When you simply stretch your limbs, I am proud that they spread farther than yesterday. When you express yourself, I am proud of your compassion. There are times I will be wrong. But I will allow you to be my teacher. I will give you what I have and be receptive to what you pour into me. I will never dim your light. Instead I will stand next to you with a matching pair of wide eyes at the wonder of how brightly that light can shine. I will carefully read every page of you and wait with bated breath for the next words you add to your story. And I will love you unconditionally with every pen stroke.

TK

STILL THE WRONG ALICE

I'm Alice. I always have been. But it seems I have always been the wrong one. First, I was wrong for my own Wonderland. Now I am wrong for yours. I've been here before. But I was hoping that if I left and decided to come back, things would be right. Things are different this time. You have built doors that I don't fit through and walls I am not tall enough to climb over. There are times they come down to meet me. But when they do, I am force-fed punishing pastries that disproportion me all over again. I look for answers everywhere. The caterpillar tells me from the beginning that his advice could be deadly. But like a fool, I listen anyway. He speaks and even though I choke on the smoke he blows, I crave his words. They are the salve for when you don't show up. I'm dying as we speak. But he makes me feel better too. The White Rabbit is late but he makes it clear that he is not coming to see me. He has plans with That Other Alice. The Right One. The one that is enough for you. The Door Mouse comes around, but I can tell she just does it to make me feel better. She pops up but offers no words, only a look of pity. There is no double talk from the Tweedles. There is just the heaviness of awkward silence because they are too polite to ask me to leave. The Cheshire Cat won't hang the moon for me. He smiles but his celestial acrobatics are for the one who deserves it. That Other Alice. The Right One. So here I sit with The Mad Hatter and The March Hare, a guest at a party that was thrown for someone else, praying for at least one impossible thing before breakfast.

TK

MIRROR

You never know it

But we are always watching you.

We see you when you laugh.

We see you when you love.

We see you when you cry.

We have our eyes on you during your most intimate moments.

When you make love, we see you.

When you sleep, we watch.

We do it all for you.

It is because we watch you live

That you get to see yourselves.

We are the mirror you need and we

Show you your souls at every angle.

If not for us, you would never know that

Your face was beautiful.

You would never know that you have

The perfect stride

Or that the ride and size of your breasts are ideal

Or that the curls of your hair rhyme with heaven

Or that the hairs of your beard are similar

In softness to an angel's wings.

We show you how to apologize.

We show you how much better you look

When you love yourselves.

Without us, history would be lost

And civilizations would crumble.

We are writers.

We are painters.

We are photographers.

We are actors.

We are singer.

We are dancers.

We are instrumentalists.

We are voyeurs.

We are mirrors.

Every day, we introduce you to yourselves.

TK

APPARITION

You meant a lot to me.
But to you, I was just another face.
Maybe not even that.
I was probably more of a whisper in the wind.
I allowed you to be a shaman.
You entranced me and summoned me
Only when it served you.
When I was ready to show you the deepest
Parts of me, you reminded me that I was
Just
A whisper...
In the wind.
I cried but you wouldn't have known.
After all, how many people pay attention
To whispers in wind?
Don't apologize.
I don't need it now.
On second thought, don't even bother to speak.
Soon, you will no longer exist to me.
It helps if you remain silent
The way ghosts of an abandoned past do.

TK

HE WAS MUSIC

He did it, Girl.

He did exactly what I said I wouldn't let him do.

He…turned….me… on.

He gave me his bebop and his hip-hop

And said, "There you go, Baby. Do with that what you will."

Just as I was figuring out how to use it,

He stunned me with the buzz of his jazz.

He let his rimshots run red hot,

Flow over me and take

Control of my soul.

His syncopation sank in and his

Rhythm began to make my backbone slip,

My hips dip and my mind trip

And I didn't even know it.

He threw in his rock 'n roll and

Busted the eardrums of my inhibitions.

His feedback, I fed back to him in waves

Of admiration.

Then he put a country twang upon that thang

And made me wanna break up, make up and

Fall in love all over again.

He had me asking myself, "Girl, what are you doing?!"

I couldn't ignore the call of his classical

Movements of mayhem down my spine.

And the raw tone of his ska

Took me to heights unknown.

I said,

"Ahhhh. Sing to me, Papa di melody uh di Rasta

As we rewrite reggae, replant roots and regrow revolution.

Right about now, I'd follow you anywhere."

Oh, I'm sorry, Girl.

I was in my own world.

You just don't know how he made me feel.

Then he put it all together and threw it at me

Until I thought my head would explode.

My toes curled,

Eyes rolled back

And I lay paralyzed.

Then he laid me down and introduced me

To the parts of my neo-soul he has just enhanced.

He owned me.

He ravaged me.

And I liked it.

TK

R*EVOL*UTION

I want to love myself in a way that no one ever has. I want it to be one of those things that is so divine that even *I* feel like there must be a catch. When I wake, I want to feel so good that I side eye myself. When I lie down, I want to feel every fiber of the sheets on my skin and to vibrate from the inside out just off the basis of my own energy. I want to have to ask myself "What do you want from me?" Even though, I know that every time the answer will be "Just be you in a way that is more magnificent than yesterday", I still want to stay in touch that way. I want to stand up and show up for myself even when no one else does. I want to face battles and go against the grain for myself. I want to never feel the need to compare myself to others and to always protect myself from that pain. I want to love myself freely and openly. I want to love myself despite everything. I want it to change the way I live. I want self-love that feels like revolution.

TK

HOW TO LOVE

Wayne said it.

I've had a lot of crooks trynna steal my heart.

 I've never really had luck,

Couldn't ever figure out how to love.

But it was supposed to be different for us. We were enrolled in those same classes. We were supposed to take the same tests along the way and work together to learn all the same lessons in love in the end. But I was the only one who showed up to class every day. You hit that chapter you couldn't understand. But instead of coming to me and asking for the notes, you let pride take over and you failed.

You became one of my moments that didn't last forever.
You left me in that corner trynna put it together.
A lot of our dreams transformed to visions.
I had to learn they weren't mistakes but piss poor decisions …about love.

You might not have had a lot of crooks trynna steal your heart.
But wanting to love honestly is just how that shit starts.
THEN how do you love?
How do you love?
I'm here in this moment I hope won't last forever.
I'm spending all my time trynna put me together.
I wanna love.
I just wanna love.

TK

* This piece was written prior to the idiocy about BLM and the 2020 election.

NOPE

I won't allow you to inspire me. I won't give you the satisfaction of allowing me to feel that same tingle in my mind that I feel all over my body when I say your name. I won't allow you to become every drop of ink from my pen and display your precious ebony to put it all to shame. I'm not gonna let your voice echo in my head and narrate every moment of pleasure. I won't acknowledge the way you have impaled my insecurities and decapitated the darkness within me and even made me smile a little bit. I am not discussing how I probably bobbed when I should have weaved because these feelings keep knocking me the hell out. I'm not gonna tell you why I'm blushing. Don't worry about why I feel so good. We're not having that discussion. So, let's just move on.

TK

DAZED & CONFUSED (THINKING IN MY GARAGE)

I don't know what I'm doing.
For years, I thought I did but that's all out the window now,
My heart was that thing I used to give the rest of me the stamina to chase after love.
I always thought my heart was pretty impressive
So, I ran with it in my hands screaming "Look at this!"
Until I was out of breath.
I would always run.
I never felt like anyone else had to run like I did.
But I thought my heart was just different that way.
I saw it as this athlete that was just *supposed* to run.
I would rest it, but I never gave it therapy.
I would take it in my hands again and just restart the race.
But now I'm confused.
I was giving my heart the rest it needed when you happened by.
You had seen me running before.
But I guess I had gotten so good at it that you didn't even notice I was doing it.
There were times you were out of breath trying to catch up.
But you still remembered our great conversations.
Even though I still had that same old heart I had been using and
Pushing to the limit, you stayed.
Eventually, I noticed I wasn't screaming anymore.
Instead, I was calmly saying "See me"
And you replied, "I always have".
So, here I am, loving openly,
Dazed and confused.
I have all this vulnerability that I never wanted and don't know what to do with.
I'm this person who feels pain at the thought of it all ending.
I am this person who gets excited when I hear from you and notices when I don't.
I'm tasting that sweet and sour flavor of my heart being idle
After falling over hurdles
But thinking it can still get up and win all by itself.
It has never been okay with having too much help.
I'm here.
With all of me engaged.
Lost.
And hoping you are just as confused as I am.

TK

ANACHRONISTIC

I am a love song, but I assure you I'm not one of those new tunes.

I don't contain incantations that will make you open

Your legs before you open your heart.

Nah. I'm not one of those.

I'm a timeless tune that repeatedly gives you the thrill

Of running to catch up with your runaway heart.

And I don't do that digital stuff.

I play on that old phonograph you have never wanted to get rid of.

I play you what is raw so that you can learn

To love all the static in my background.

There is no grinding to my melody.

When I play, you sweep your lover into your arms and

Wish I would never end.

I am sweet and gentle, but there is sorrow in me.

That sorrow is because they don't write them like me anymore.

I always play solo.

But I play boldly because it is the only way I know.

Through every window, I make myself known—

Never out of sync, but forever out of time.

TK

HOME

I came home today and only you were here.
You're always here.
But today was different.
Usually you sit off somewhere in a corner.
You aren't usually the focal point.
I can usually look at the pieces of me that lie on my couch
When I should really be gathering them and
Placing them neatly on my therapist's couch to allow
Them to be properly deconstructed.
I can usually get distracted by the light from the face
Of my cell phone when I get a call from that man
Who is no good for me.
Then my focus shifts to the pitter patter of my heart
That I never noticed until that moment because
After all, nothing ever happened for me until it happened
On his time.
I can usually distract myself by agonizing over the stories
I have been given that I don't always recognize as gifts
Because how dare I have the audacity to write them?
I can usually keep myself busy sending birthday texts
And doing welfare checks on people who never think of me.
On those calls, I can focus on not letting my insides
Scream out loud.
I can usually look at all of my clothes and complain
That I have nothing to wear
When the real problem is, I really long for someone
I can be safely naked with.
I have spent a lot of time pushing those things aside.
I pushed and pulled them so far into corners
That they ended up on the lawn.
Today, Myself, I came home to just you.
I've lived with you before.
But now that it's just us, I want to learn to love you too.

TK

BLACK

Black is the absence of color.
But my Black doesn't fit that definition the way you think.
See, **MY** Black is more of the "absorption of all light" sort.
That means **MY** Black holds everything
And it doesn't need what you have to be beautiful.
MY Black is what you see when you turn off the lights.
It stops you in your tracks and makes you think hard
About your next move.
MY Black is the night.
It is the cloak of comfort that drapes over you after
A hard day's work.
MY Black is essential.
It goes with everything.
MY Black is oil and coal.
It fuels everything you have.
You might say **MY** Black is the absence of color.
But that makes it the reference point that taught you what
Colors were in the first place.
The black you know might be the absence of light,
A stain
Or a bruise.
But you can keep that black for yourself.
I don't need it.
It isn't mine.

TK

SLOW DANCE

You were both my heaven and hell.
I kinda laid on clouds decorated in razor blades
When you were around.
I told you how I felt when they drew blood but
You were most comfortable with the stories about
Your soft words upon my skin.
We slow danced between darkness and light but
It wasn't until the song ended that I realized
The burning room we twirled around in was
One of my own design.
Initially I meant it as a sanctuary for us but the embers
From your gaslight were far too much to bear.
At the moment you stopped dancing and started
To recite those same speeches,
I decided to save myself.
My phone still rings
But I never call those old feelings back.
Now that I am dancing alone,
I never have to worry about anyone stepping on my feet
Or swaying out of sync.
I can hear the words of the song now
And I realize it was always written for me.
It can go on forever and I'll just keep dancing.
I really don't think I will ever get tired.

TK

LEAR

I want to leave the way King Lear did—

Silently and without commotion.

When my "She dies" is written,

There will be no need for overt pomp and circumstance

Because there will have been an abundance throughout my life.

I will leave my kingdom to my daughters without contest

But my Cordelias will be my favorites.

They will have found no need to compete

For my affection and know that nothing they could ever say

Would rival the love they showed me as I walked beside them.

My Cordelias—my strong, reflective, silent, genuine types—

Will be the perfect queens.

In my fifth and final act,

There might be tears.

But I want the tears to weaken against the

Joy in a smile I have given

The peace in the words I have written

The love in an embrace I have given

The comfort in a kiss I have left.

I want no prolonged grief but the celebration of

My life and my example.

I want it all to be said and done at

"She dies."

TK

What do you want to be your legacy? What would you like to leave behind/be known for?

www.ingramcontent.com/pod-product-compliance
Lightning Source LLC
Chambersburg PA
CBHW061747290426

44108CB00028B/2916